Creative Circle Time Lessons for the Early Years

Yvonne Weatherhead

SAGE

Los Angeles • London • New Delhi • Singapore • Washington DC

SAGE Publications
1 Oliver's Yard
55 City Road
London EC1Y 1SP

SAGE Publications Inc.
2455 Teller Road
Thousand Oaks, California 91320

SAGE Publications India Pvt Ltd
B 1/I 1 Mohan Cooperative Industrial Area
Mathura Road, Post Bag 7
New Delhi 110 044

SAGE Publications Asia-Pacific Pte Ltd
33 Pekin Street #02-01
Far East Square
Singapore 048763

www.luckyduck.co.uk

Illustrators: **Andrew Chubb**
 Janine Tracey (for Dabbit Day)

Library of Congress Control Number 2008935010

British Library Cataloguing in Publication data
A catalogue record for this book is available from the British Library

ISBN 978-1-4129-3533-3

Typeset by C & M Digitals (P) Ltd., Chennai, India
Printed in India at Replika Pvt. Ltd
Printed on paper from sustainable resources

Creative Circle Time Lessons
for the Early Years

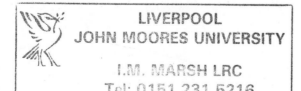
A Lucky Duck Book

Circle Time is...

Collective responsibility

Individual and group responses

Realistic problem solving

Caring and supportive atmospheres

Laughter and sometimes tears

Enjoying the challenge

Time for ourselves

Interesting and innovative ideas

Meaningful games

Escapism...

This book is dedicated to the following people for their help and support over the years:

Rod – For our love of Italy and your everlasting hopes for the future

Chloe, Robert and Jamie – For your success, I am proud of you all

William Rusby – my dad – For your musical influence and love of books

Mary Rusby – my mum – For your love and support always

Alison – For being my best friend – you're a star

Irene and Judi Weatherhead – For your support with making Stripy bear

Nic, Tom and Charlotte for the fun we have…

Di and Pat for a well deserved relaxation in Spain

Gail – For your support, friendship and encouragement always

Lauren and James – Wonderful niece and nephew

Uncle Tom – For always being there to support us all

Marland Hill School staff, children, governors and parents – To wish us continued success in our new school

Peter Millray – For your continued enthusiastic support

Sandra Goulden – For being so patient… I couldn't have written this book without you

Contents

About the Author

Yvonne Weatherhead has been the headteacher of Marland Hill Community Primary School in Rochdale for eighteen years and has led the school through three very successful Ofsted inspections. Her contributions to leadership and management in the inspections were deemed as "outstanding" and "very strong." Yvonne has also been the federation headteacher of two schools and found this to be a very successful and rewarding experience. Marland Hill is also a lead school in behaviour management and serves a socially disadvantaged community. It has recently been rebuilt as a purpose built resource base school to develop an inclusive approach with a hearing impaired unit and has an additional visually impaired drop-in rainbow room for under 5's. Marland Hill has received the Silver Artsmark Award for contributions to Dance, Drama, Art and Music and is a Leading Literacy School for Rochdale Local Authority.

Yvonne has for many years led enthusiastic in-service training in Circle Time, behaviour management and literacy throughout the country. Yvonne's first book to be published by Lucky Duck was *Enriching Circle Time: Dream Journeys and Pasitive Thoughts*. This latest book, Creative Circle Time Lessons for the Early Years, links Circle Time lessons to the teaching of the Literacy Curriculum, which has always been encouraged by Yvonne and has enhanced the teaching of oracy skills.

Music, dance, movement and drama are used as a stimulus in all of her books. Yvonne's enthusiasm for the arts has encouraged many school visitors to comment favourably on the creative and lively approach to the teaching of music and the lively interactive assemblies.

An Introduction to the 26 Lessons in this Book

Teachers lives are so busy! I should know, I have been involved in Education for 30 years and I still find I am chasing my tail to complete all my tasks. So how can I help you to effectively organise a yearly programme of exciting Circle Time lessons?

This book has been developed around 26 alphabetical themes, centralised around a lovable character of a bear, which you can purchase or make for yourself, and personalise by choosing your own name for it. There are four main strands to the book, which are linked to the Social Skills curriculum and enhance the themes of:

- Self-esteem
- Relationships
- Communication
- Spiritual and Moral Development.

The strands are developed throughout the 26 themes by the carefully planned Circle Time lessons written in alphabetical order, with a weekly introduction of a new poem and rhythm to accompany the poem. All the lessons have been well trialled by both myself and other Circle Time users, and have proved to be very popular and a great source of excitement for the children. The children often meet me at breakfast club just to ask, "Is it Circle Time today, we love it!" The children also take part regularly in In-Service programmes, presented by myself and staff, where these skills are developed and demonstrated.

Circle Time enhances children's confidence in speaking and listening and at my present school this has been developed to a very high level. The school is in a socially deprived area and at a recent Inspection under the 'New Ofsted Framework', children's 'Development and Well being' and 'Care, Guidance and Support' received 'Outstanding' grades. A quote from the report stated that, 'Dream Journey assemblies develop children's imaginations and self beliefs.' A further quote, 'Children's spiritual, moral, social and cultural development is promoted extremely well.' The comments refer to the many supporting programmes we have in place, which are further enhanced by our structured creative Circle Time sessions.

Whether you are a confident Circle Time practitioner or a novice, this book should be accessible to you and be easy to use. The notes on 'How to use this book' will explain how to access the information needed. As your Circle Time develops you will be able to notice how your children develop in confidence and self-esteem. Your children will develop a supportive and trusting network which helps all individuals to discuss issues and problems. These materials have been described by people who have trialled them as, "A very exciting practical resource, easy to use and built on a very solid foundation of many years of expertise and practice."

I hope you enjoy using the resources, have fun and learn from your children's many contributions to each weekly alphabetical delight!

Yvonne Weatherhead

1

How to Use this Book

This book has been written for both experienced and inexperienced Circle Time practitioners. To make it easily accessible to the teacher for each lesson you will need the following resources.

Firstly, a *CD* is enclosed which has images of the poems and bears for each letter of the alphabet. These need to be printed and copied on to A3 or A4 paper and laminated.

The poems and letters are written in alphabetical order and introduced on a weekly basis to the children. To aid visual stimulation for the children, *A3* and *A4 posters* can be reproduced to display the letters in alphabetical order around the classroom. These can therefore be referred to on a regular basis, in Literacy and Circle Time lessons.

The teacher needs to *purchase a bear*, to be used throughout the Circle Time lessons. The bear's name could be chosen by the class, but it is important that it is a two syllable name, to fit in with the rhythm of the poems. In the poems, all the bears' names begin with 'B', to enhance the idea of an alliteration with the word bear. For example, Brindle bear and Bradley bear. In this book, all the bears are male, as the reference in the poems are to a male bear, as he is described as 'king bear'.

Also included is a *knitting pattern*, so that 'Stripy' bear can be reproduced. The purchase or making of a bear is a very important part of the Circle Time session, as he becomes a 'real character' to discuss issues linked to the social skills curriculum. Furthermore, children often talk 'through' the bear, as he is passed around the circle, for 'rounds' and other games.

A *CD of music* is also enclosed to recite each alphabetical poem to. On the CD there is an example of how to recite the poem to a rhythm followed by just the rhythm to recite it as a class. It is advisable that each teacher keeps a *box of instruments* in the classroom to enable rhythms to be played simultaneously to the poem being recited. It is usually more helpful when a third of the class use the instruments to enable the poem to be recited, as well as the rhythm played to accompany the performance.

This book aims to encourage teachers to use the 26 alphabetical lesson notes with a flexible approach across the curriculum, either for a specific social skills curriculum or linked to a Literacy lesson. It is accompanied with poems and rhythms (on a CD) which can be used effectively in Literacy lessons to encourage and develop speaking, listening and performance skills. The Circle Time ideas can also be included in Personal, Social, Citizenship and Health Education lessons (PSCHE). Furthermore, this approach enhances the music curriculum with its focus on rhythm, use of instrumentation and performance skills.

Before each Circle Time session the children should be encouraged to listen to an alphabetical poem on the music CD and to follow the words of the poem or song. In the first lesson the bear puppet should be introduced to the children and should be named and be part of all the Circle Time activities. The poems and songs should usually be performed in the classroom before the circle is formed. The children are encouraged to read the poem and use instruments to accompany the rhythm of the poem. The CD has rhythms to accompany each poem and music to accompany the songs. Following this, the children recite the poem and also use instruments to enhance the poem. The majority of poems can be learned off by heart very quickly and children enjoy the challenge of this, which results in a presentation and performance with instrumentation. This part of the lesson could be introduced at a different time to the Circle Time session, for example, as part of a Literacy lesson, or at the beginning of a morning session to support reading activities or oracy skills. The same poem and alphabetical letter is used throughout the week.

The Circle Time lesson activities proceed following the weekly introduction of the poem. This is often on a Monday morning. The poems are purposefully written in alphabetical order to encourage the children to continue to use and become confident with the alphabet in a fun but challenging way. Many words end in 'ing', for example, **dancing and hiding**; this supports the teaching of 'ing' in the Literacy curriculum. There are also some simple words like **wow**, **tall**, **very happy** and some challenging words, such as **noughts and crosses, adorable, ice-cream and laughing**. The 'm' in the centre of the book encourages the children to associate **M is for mending bear**. The children should be told that **M also** mends the two parts of the alphabet together, so it is remembered as the middle letter of the alphabet.

Games can be played with words that come before and after the chosen alphabetical letters and the different words in the bear's alphabet. It is always a good idea to spend a few sessions going through the order of the words on the posters so that the children can become familiar with the order of the alphabetical words. The children enjoy the words to be used in an alphabetical challenge to see how many they can remember. If the words are cut into strips the Alphabetical game can be played from the circle. This game is shown at the beginning of the 26 themed lessons in Chapter 8 where the alphabetical word strips are also included. The alphabetical word strips are included on the CD.

How to begin Circle Time

For Circle Time to be most effective, a whole school approach needs to be established where it is clearly understood the deeper foundations of mutual respect, care for all individuals and trust that leads to a feeling of security. Schools need to take the time to establish these foundations at all levels, as a strong pastoral support programme within schools strengthens relationships and enables them to become honest and secure.

Circle Time should be planned across the school to ensure the continuity and progression of skills across the Key Stages supports the progress of the Personal, Social, Citizenship and Health Education programme. My own belief is that time should be given on the timetable to ensure that Circle Time is a structured part of your working week. Ideally, it should begin as a short session on a Monday morning where the week's timetable, targets or procedures need to be revisited and then later in the week a more structured timetable of Circle Time themes needs to be established. A Circle Time lesson should normally last between 15–30 minutes for Foundation Stage and Key Stage 1.

In the ideal classroom, Monday morning needs to be a place of regaining tranquillity, where the children come in to peaceful music, sit in their place or on the carpet with a book or activity, and relax into the situation before beginning any more structured work. Relaxation and breathing techniques are often a good opener to the week, or a relaxing poem, or piece of music. Beginnings of days or a week are an ideal time to use the positive thoughts in this book, as a stimulating activity to begin your week. These positive thoughts should be read and reflected upon through discussion.

Circle Time Organisation

Sitting in a circle enables children to feel a sense of equality and helps them to be responsible and able to make important decisions. The circle is a symbol of co-operation and support for each other.

Some Circle Time writers feel it should be a circle of chairs ... personally, I do not feel it matters. It is important however, that every child has a place to sit that is not too squashed, so that if they change places, there is an obvious space to go to. Some teachers like to use carpet tiles for this purpose.

The teacher's role is one of co-ordinator or facilitator where they create a supportive atmosphere and take part in all activities.

The benefits to children are...

- children have a sense of belonging to a group they can trust
- it encourages good communication and co-operation skills
- it promotes positive self-esteem and behaviour
- children begin to understand and value themselves and others
- it aids the development of positive relationships with each other
- it encourages self-discipline
- it develops confidence in speaking and ensures children are good listeners.

It helps children to...

- discuss sensitive issues
- resolve conflicts
- solve problems
- be able to participate in reflection and meditation/ dream journeys.

Rules

It is important to establish some very clear but specific rules for all the children follow in Circle Time. These are applicable for Foundation Stage, Key Stage 1 and Key Stage 2 children.

An object such as a bear or puppet, instrument, soft toy, or shell should be passed round to initiate talk and to give the child the right to talk. Children must signal with their hands if they wish to speak.

There should be no put downs and the exploration of put downs should be dealt with early on in Circle Time.

Children are told that good behaviour is expected throughout the Circle Time sessions, and a discussion of expectations on good behaviour would be beneficial.

A child has the right to pass if he/she is not able to speak. This child may then speak at the end if he/she wishes to. If a child continually does this deliberately they may be asked to sit outside the circle until they are ready to rejoin the group (unless the child has particular difficulties). A discussion with the child after the session about positive expectations on how to participate would be helpful.

A teacher has the right to sit a child outside the circle if they break any of the rules explained to them. The teacher must find a quick opportunity to enable the child to return to the circle, e.g. "You are sitting beautifully now John, join our circle".

No one in the circle must be named in a negative way. The child must say "Someone has hit me." Family names are also respected and 'Someone' must be used, not Mum, Dad, brother, etc.

Very private concerns should be encouraged for problem boxes.

Circle Time Rules Should be Simple for Children

- We listen to each other
- We may pass
- There are no put downs
- We do not tell anyone else what they should be doing
- When we try to help we say, "Do you think it would be helpful if..."
- We behave well and tell the truth
- We speak by raising our hand or by using the bear or puppet

TWO CDS accompany this book:

Audio CD

On the audio CD, each poem or song is read or sung by primary aged children, to demonstrate how it should be performed. Following the performance, a rhythm or song will be played, so each teacher with their group of children can 'have a go' without the help of the children on the CD.

The majority of the alphabetical words are poems, with the exception of Goalkeeper bear, Laughing bear and Stripy bear, which are all songs. King bear, which is the most serious of all the poems, is read without a rhythm. Children can be encouraged to read this 'out loud' to try and replicate a 'majestic' and important feel to it. Microphones can be useful to assist with this process.

CD Rom

The CD Rom contains the following:

- All the poems, including the appropriate bear, for each letter of the alphabet
- Outline images of all bears labelled with correct alphabetical name,
  e.g. Baloo bear, Bathtime bear
- The alphabet strips, for the alphabet game (see Chapter 8) including the picture of bears on each strip.
- The knitting pattern for the bear
- The story script of Dabbit Day, including images of the story (see Very happy bear)
- Positive Thought scripts with appropriate alphabetical bear
- Circle Time notice board poster with appropriate bear
- A4 list of Bazal's stripes in order

2

Typical Circle Time Activities

Warm-ups

Use fun warm-ups to help the children to relax. Sometimes this might be a highly energetic game involving movement and changing places.

Rounds

A round is also a good way to start Circle Time. These can include lots of unfinished sentences, e.g.

> When I grow up I want to be…
> If I could float and be as light as a bubble I would…
> The best surprise I ever had was…
> The thing that made me laugh the most was…

Discussion/Problem Solving

The Rounds can also be used to solve problems, followed by an 'Open Discussion' where children may say, "I need help because…". The children in the circle may indicate by raising their hands to help and say, "Would it help if…"

Following this, and after thanking each child's contribution, it is important to write or think through a quick action plan or keep a diary of ways to solve problems. These diaries can be re-looked at when problems reoccur. (Often a big book of problems and solutions is the best way to record this). The 'Open Discussion' questions could come from the problem box you have in your classroom (see the problem box section Chapter 4).

A technique often used in Circle Time is for children to be put in pairs or 3's to discuss ideas. These ideas could relate to any area of the curriculum and is a particularly good resource for:

- Humanities issues, e.g. resolving conflicts
- Spiritual and moral issues, e.g. Friendships, caring for others
- Problems of bullying, racist and sexist issues
- What should we do if…? How would we feel if…?

Activities

Game: this can also be used as a 'brain break' in normal classroom activities, linked to accelerated learning.

This can be done collectively or in groups. e.g. As a group, in ten seconds make a : Bridge, boat, letter 'S', peeled banana, a working machine, production line, holiday scene.

Activity: Round Style

This can be done as a whole group:

(a) Name game: My name is Janet.
My name is Paul and this is Janet.
My name is Bazal and this is Paul and Janet.

(b) Child one: I went to market and I bought a ball.
Child two: I went to market and I bought a ball and a bat.
Child three: I went to market and I bought a ball, a bat, and some chocolate.

The game continues round the circle.

(c) Click and name game, i.e. Slap thighs (two hands), clap hands together, click one finger and thumb and then click the other. On the clicks, say name, e.g. Click 1 'Pe'; Click 2 'ter' (Peter). Next person then says name on clicks and pass it on. All members of group participate with slap thighs, clap hands and click together. Using same actions, pass on a favourite food, favourite drink or favourite pastime. Very good for co-ordination skills.

Activity: Game Style

This can be done as a whole group:

(a) Roll a ball to make a statement and roll it to someone else and invite another person to make a statement also. Keep the ball moving across the Circle.

Examples:

- My favourite place is... McDonalds, the cinema, the park
- Use it for Literacy or Numeracy activities
- List all the verbs (doing words) you can think of
- Times tables, Add on a number or take away a number.

(b) Now throw or pass a ball of string to someone who continues a statement (hold on to the first part of the string). e.g. My favourite toy is... Hopefully, by the end of the game an interesting web will have been woven, as well as having lots of fun!

Energiser

Group yell

As it sounds, not recommended if you are going to scare the whole school! Children and teacher pat thighs and say the word quietly and then louder and louder and, at the end with instructions of '1, 2, 3', jump high and shout the word out very loudly!

Example yell: **Happy**   **Surprise**   **Bubbles**   **Thunderstorms**

Another possibility is a group chant with playing of musical instruments softer and then louder to a crescendo (or in reverse). Energiser can also be a changing places game:

The boats carry you across the sea ...

One child stands in the middle of the circle and says, "The boats carry you across the sea if you are wearing blue". All children wearing blue have to change places and the child in the centre of the circle needs to try and sit in another space so there is someone new in the middle. Alternatively, you can play *The Boats Stop at the Lighthouse if you...* and as the children cross the circle they shake hands or hug someone.

Positive Thoughts

Positive Thoughts are located at the end of the following alphabet sections and are themed as below:

B – Feeling special.	S – Our fun journey to school.
C – Feeling relaxed.	T – Happy thoughts.
H – Something that makes you smile.	U – A field of golden buttercups.
K – Somebody you would like to help.	V – A favourite day with friend.
L – Making yourself laugh.	W – 'WOW' words for special things.
M – Positive Thoughts about a friend.	X – A wish for something good to happen to someone who needs it.
N – Being 'on top of the world'.	Y – Good dreams.
Q – A secret place to feel relaxed.	
R – Music that makes you feel relaxed.	

These thoughts can be used at the beginning or end of a day or Circle Time session. They are aimed at encouraging children in self-awareness and positive self-esteem and also encourage children to have the confidence to:

• Stay as healthy as possible
• Keep themselves and others safe
• Have worthwhile and fulfilling relationships
• Develop independence and responsibility
• Make the most of their own and others' abilities.

Children use the focus for the week to keep them feeling very positive about themselves and others. They are able to interpret the focus, for example, 'Feeling relaxed', verbally, artistically and in written form. They are also able to share their ideas with others and to learn from their friends, positive ideas to use for themselves.

Circle Time Notice Board

Put up a notice board connected with the Circle Time themes. Encourage the children to bring in pictures, poems, stories and photographs connected with the theme of the week. Write a message to parents telling them the themes of the week, e.g. 'Party bear' and try to involve them in Circle Time. See if they can bring in party photographs of their children, or ideas for party games and food, for others to learn from.

Write a list for other parents of great birthday party day's out, e.g. bowling, roller skating, a visit to a park, etc.

Always put the notice board at the children's height and ensure parents know where their notices will be written and you will soon see how interactive it becomes!

Circle Time Notice Board

Think about your favourite place.
Draw or write about it, or have you got a
photograph to show us?
Tell us why it is your favourite place.
How does it make you feel to be there?
Stick your pictures, photographs or writing
on our Circle Time Notice Board.

Thank you for sharing your favourite place
with all of us.

Once children begin to use this notice board on their own, it can be a feature, at the beginnings or endings of some days, for the teacher and children to look at the new additions to the board. It is great fun to do and becomes a class focus, linking home and school.

Dream journeys

Dream journeys are creative visualisations and are described in full in Chapter 5.

Useful Tips on How to Perform a Circle Time Lesson

Each lesson in the book can be copied on to card and is written in the following format:

An introduction

Opening round game or warm-ups (there may be two sections here).

Main feature

Linked usually to the lesson objective, at this point, the lesson objective should be introduced to the children in 'child' speak, e.g. Bathtime bear. "We are going to help each other to solve problems and to discuss how we feel when a problem happens." The main feature could be a game, discussion or problem solving activity.

Additional ideas

These are extra activities to support the Circle Time theme. They could be a song, activity, round, etc.

Lesson ending

This could be a game, energiser, dream journey, song, round, etc.

I have found it easier to cut-up each lesson note with individual activities into strips and number the cards in order. They can then be used as manageable cards on the floor in front of you and enable you to facilitate the lesson far more easily (the numbers are helpful in case you drop them, believe me, it happens a lot, especially when being observed!).

If an activity takes longer than expected, or the children extend ideas in an interesting way, it is easy to miss out some smaller activities by moving the card to the back of the pile. This card can then be revisited at a later date.

The cards can then be filed in a box, similar to a storage box for photographs. Section the box using the headings in this chapter, i.e. Introduction (which include games or warm-ups), Main feature (which include discussions and problem solving), Additional ideas (which could be songs, rounds or activities) and finally Lesson ending (which could be games, energiser or dream journeys).

At a future date it is possible to have a 'favourites day' and to mix up the activities, or just simply use one section if you have a spare minute in the day.

The Circle Time activities in this book have been written in alphabetical order and each lesson can be taught in sequence. However, as each lesson has a separate lesson objective, the lessons can be taught out of sequence. If necessary, the only challenge for the teacher is to ensure they keep a record of the strands of Self-Esteem, Communication, Relationships and Spiritual and Moral Development that are being taught in a term (see Chapter 6) to ensure there is breadth and balance of the components needed to be taught.

At the beginning of each term it is often important to remind the children the rules of Circle Time (see Chapter 1).

A suggested alphabetical format for each term would be as follows:

Term 1:   A–I
Term 2:   J–R
Term 3:   S–Z

It is also important for PSCHE co-ordinators to look at the continuity and progression of skills in Circle Time across the school. For this purpose, a scheme of work has been suggested in Chapter 6 linking it to the Citizenship scheme of work in Key Stage One.

Furthermore, in Chapter 6 planning sheets have been suggested to enable you to be accountable for Ofsted purposes, with the link to the Citizenship scheme of work. These should be written with reference notes only (this can be done in 10 minutes), ticking off the objectives to be achieved – these appear on the reverse of the sheet and on the top for cross-referencing. There are two different types of planning sheet, Foundation Stage and Key Stage One. All sheets have the relevant objectives attached. There is a space for an evaluation (no more than 5 minutes writing!) and also spaces for adaptations if the lesson moves in a different direction as a result of the child's input or your decision to spend longer on a section. It should be emphasised that using the numbered strips of cards is the easier approach when facilitating a lesson.

The planning sheets in this book can be put into your planning file with annotated notes written to evaluate how the lesson has progressed – these can be written down the side. It is not necessary to use the other planning sheets, they are there if you feel they are more explicit for accountability purposes, or required at your present school.

A scheme of work is written in the QCA Citizenship folder (pp. 21–25), and these themes can be developed using continuity and progression of skills across the age groups. Schools can also develop their own schemes of work, ensuring these skills are covered effectively. The themes can be placed with the new Excellence and Enjoyment material and the Social and Emotional Aspects of Learning (SEAL scheme of work).

The skills that need to be taught include:

Key Stage One

Developing confidence and responsibility and making the most of their abilities

1. Pupils should be taught:

   a. to recognise what they like and dislike, what is fair and unfair, and what is right and wrong
   b. to share their opinions on things that matter to them and explain their views to recognise, name and deal with their feelings in a positive way.

Preparing to play an active role as citizens

2. Pupils should be taught:

    a. to take part in discussions with one other person and the whole class
    b. to take part in a simple debate about topical issues
    c. to recognise choices they can make, and recognise the differences between right and wrong
    d. that they belong to various groups and communities, such as family and school.

Developing good relationships and respecting the differences between people

3. Pupils should be taught:

    a. to recognise how their behaviour affects other people
    b. to listen to other people, and play and work co-operatively
    c. to identify and respect the differences and similarities between people.

How to Develop Materials

The following section is divided into further effective ideas to be brought to Circle Time sessions. It particularly looks at:

- Problem solving boxes, encouraging children to play an active role as responsible citizens. It also encourages good relationships and respecting the similarities and differences between people
- Making people feel special, by choosing selected children to be a 'Superstar' of the week
- The use of calming techniques and smaller circles to encourage the solving of specific problems.

Problem boxes

The use of problem boxes is a very effective tool within the classroom to enable the teacher and children to discuss problems with relationships, health and safety issues, individual worries and school worries. The Circle Time session can be engineered by the teacher to devise solutions to problems using a step-by-step approach. The circle of children should become a very supportive and caring group, who try and build confidence in each other when problems occur, by helping solve the problems.

The teacher's role in the Early Years is usually to write the problems and to encourage the children to think of ways to solve them. Children often like to solve these problems through the media of a bear or puppet, or in a role-play situation. The teacher may also ask the bear or puppet to help solve the problems.

Children are not encouraged to name family members or other children within Circle Time sessions. More personal or private problems are dealt with on a one-to-one with the teacher and child.

To enable children to value the problem box it has a different theme in each year group, the following are suggested progressive age-related approaches.

Nursery/Reception

A magic postbag can be kept in a special part of the classroom, accompanied by a post person's hat – for a role-play situation. The teacher puts problems and school scenarios in the magic postbag, e.g:

- Zarina is lonely and has no one to play with at playtime. How can we help her?
- Paul does not like staying at school at lunchtime. How can we help him? How can we cheer him up?
- Winnie the Pooh is new to school and feels lonely. How can we help him?

A special weekly post person's delivery is made as part of a role-play situation for children. A child is dressed up in the post person's hat and given the postbag to deliver to the circle of children in Circle Time. The teacher reads out the problem and asks the children to help with solving the problem. A post person's hat is passed round the circle to try and help solve the problem. Each child wears the hat in turn and tries to help solve the problem.

Year One

A large barrel or tub is kept in the classroom with polystyrene pieces in it. The teacher puts in problems, helped by the children's ideas, during each week. They are written on coloured cards (i.e. library card size). At Circle Time the children select a problem by putting their hand in the barrel or tub and giving it to the teacher. The teacher and children then try and solve the problem.

A bear could be passed round the circle to help the children to talk through. When they receive the bear they can try and solve the problem. Alternatively, a bear may be put in the centre of the circle for the children to talk through. They may volunteer to come and give a solution to the problem. They may use the words, "Would it help if…"

Year Two

An owl can be displayed in the classroom with a postbag hanging from its beak (Harry Potter style). Children's problems are put into the postbag, on card, throughout the week. A child may ask the teacher to include a problem in the bag or the problems could be teacher initiated. All problems are anonymous. At a weekly Circle Time session, a selected child then carries the owl and postbag into the circle, or for dramatic effect, the owl could be lowered from the ceiling to fly into the lesson (quite easy to do really!). The teacher then encourages the children to try and solve the problems and find solutions to help each other. To make this session even more effective, the children also like this session to be linked to 'bubble burst'.

Bubble Burst

Bubbles are introduced to the children as a calming effect, bubbles are blown into the circle and children are asked how the bubbles make them feel. The children are then told that 'Bubble burst' will be an important part of the Circle Time session.

They are told that as they pass the bubbles round the circle, as each child blows a bubble into the air, they help blow into the air any small worries they have. Each child is asked to follow with their eyes their own bubbles into the air and, as they get higher and higher, to feel as light as a feather and relaxed as the bubble. They can pretend that their problem is inside the bubble and as it bursts, the problem seems small and lighter.

Children can discuss which problems could be blown away easily. These can include, being cross with someone, falling out with a friend or being afraid of something. Sometimes it is helpful to tell the children to use a pretend bubble around them when someone calls them a horrible name. As the name is said, the bubble stops it hurting them – it can't get through to upset them. In fact, the words could bounce off the bubble (these methods are often called 'anger spoilers').

Children need to be reminded if it is a bigger problem they must discuss it with their teacher or a family member.

This means the teacher will talk privately to a child about a problem they may have. Children should be seen at playtime or dinnertime, and be made to feel the problem is very private and confidential. Children are always told the truth, but supported throughout.

Where a teacher feels a problem needs to be shared with another professional or adult, the child is told by the teacher they may need extra help in solving this problem (e.g. in cases of child abuse, etc.). In all cases, a child must feel that confidentiality is very important and only professionals who have expertise in this field will be consulted. Teachers involved in any of these cases must follow the local, Child Protection guidelines. In the exceptional case that a child reveals an allegation in Circle Time, the teacher must immediately stop any further discussion on the issue and ask the child sensitively to come and discuss that particular issue with the teacher privately. In my wide experience, children very rarely reveal highly sensitive issues in Circle Time sessions.

Problem solving strategies

Problem solving strategies are often outlined to the children in a simple ladder format:

Ladder Format	Example problem
1. Decide on the problem	1. e.g. I have no-one to play with
2. Think of why the problem is occurring	2. (a) Only like playing with one other friend (b) Like playing physical games, e.g. ball games, skipping
3. Think of a solution	3. (a) Discuss as a class likes and dislikes at playtime (b) Make a sociograph of who likes playing different games
4. Follow through the solution	4. Link friends or social groups of children playing together at playtime
5. Review the problem and solution	5. Discuss with children one week later how playtime is going. Have mentors to help children play together

Children are also given the opportunity to put a variety of bubble shapes in the postbag which may just have:

Making people feel special

Encourage children to bring in their photograph or, an even better idea, take photographs with a digital camera of all the children at the beginning of the year and display them all on a SUPERSTARS board:

- Choose one child each week to be the special 'Superstar'
- Encourage all the children to write or say a positive statement about the 'Special Child'
- During that week let the child have privileges and feel really special
- Ensure all children have their special week during the school year.

Use Circle Time to reinforce positive statements about the child. Send the child out of the circle while the class say positive statements about that child. Return the child back to the circle and present them with a scroll of positive statements. Tie it up with a ribbon to make it special.(You could also have a 'Special Member of Staff' board in the staffroom, very good for promoting self-esteem. You could continue with their likes and dislikes, including room for their favourite poem).

Smaller purposeful circles

Sometimes having smaller circles for those children who need more encouragement to talk is useful. Circles of eight to ten children usually work well to achieve more effective purposeful circles and these are specifically helpful for Key Stage 1 and Foundation Stage children and children with Special Needs, including behavioural difficulties. They can also support children who have English as an additional language, when role models are used to support the teaching of the acquisition of English. Smaller circles could be grouped and regrouped to tackle different situations.

Use your Headteacher to have 'time out' with a special group! Use bubble lamps and water features to create a lovely calm atmosphere.

Use your Teaching Assistants to support small groups with specific targeted children, these groups may consist of six children.

Dream Journeys in Key Stage One and the Foundation Stage

Dream journeys are a creative visualisation where children listen to, visualise and relax into a story being read to them. On occasions, the dream journey can take the place of an idea with the accompaniment of music. The stories read to younger children should be introducing relaxation techniques of lying or sitting down with their eyes closed or concentrating on a bubble lamp or listening to quiet music. They should begin to teach the children how to use their senses of seeing, hearing, touching, tasting and smelling. The stories should appeal to these senses, but also some should just be about the concentration on the use of relaxation techniques. The dream journeys should fill their minds with ideas and images (visual learners). At first some children are only able to listen to the story (auditory learners). These dream journeys can be extended into art work, dance and drama and creative writing in Literacy (kinesthetic learners).

In this book there are seven dream journeys which can be repeated with children to ensure they pick up the techniques of relaxation. It is always useful to practise one process a few times, so they understand what is required of them. The themes cover the following:

- Adorable: Favourite places, What can you see, hear and do? Feeling special
- Cooling: Lying by a pond in the sunshine, listening to sounds, feeling the sun's rays
- Energetic: Imagining cloud gazing, creating shapes and images
- Goalkeeper: Relaxation techniques with body, including breathing exercises
- Noughts and crosses: Fairground excitement, winning and losing. Fairness and justice
- Relaxing: Use of music to create own creative visualisation of a painting
- Umbrella: A nature walk, use of all five senses.

One model approach to dream journeys

Children should be sitting or lying in a place which feels supportive and calm, either in a circle or in a space in the hall or classroom.Children should be told to "Sit or lie in a relaxed position. Put your hands on your knees (for sitting position), by your side (for lying position). Are you all comfortable? (Praise good sitting or lying positions!). Well done everybody, now you can close your eyes."

Say to the children, "Breathe in slowly and out slowly. Remember to keep your eyes closed and just listen to your breathing. Now wriggle your fingers, then relax them and let them be still. Now move your head slowly from side to side and now relax it and be still. Well done! Now we are ready to listen to our story."

Children should be read the dream journey or relaxation techniques. Children are told, "Listen to the story and see if you can see the pictures of the story in your mind. See if you can use your

senses. What can you see, touch, taste, smell and hear? Well done everyone for keeping your eyes closed! We are ready to start our dream journey"

A dream journey or relaxation technique is read to the children. If it is a relaxation technique, the children will be expected to do it as you read it slowly. Keep encouraging the children for the relaxation techniques with, "Well done. That's really good." Read the stories slowly and pause where you think it needs a bit of thought. Some children find it difficult to keep their eyes closed, but if a child opens their eyes, unless they are being a distraction, ignore it and praise the rest of the group.

At the end of the dream journey, remind the children to breathe slowly and listen to their own quiet breathing. Tell them "Breathe in and out slowly and feel relaxed. Now wriggle your fingers then relax them and let them be still. Now move your head slowly from side to side and now relax it and be still. When you are ready, open your eyes. Well done everyone. You listened really well".

At the end of the session, give the children a few moments to get used to their surroundings before you ask them questions about their journey. See how many children could really visualise the story and work on the skills with others to build up for the future.

Dream journeys are explained in further detail in *Enriching Circle Time: Dream Journeys and Positive Thoughts* (Yvonne Weatherhead, Lucky Duck 2004).

Circle Time Planning Linked to Citizenship: 5–7 year olds

Planning

A Scheme of Work has been planned for Circle Time activities to encompass the four main strands of Circle Time and to show where to fit in elements of the Citizenship Scheme of Work. Many Circle Time writers recognise the four main strands to consider are:

- Self-esteem
- Communication
- Relationships
- Spiritual and Moral Development.

These four strands are split into three termly themes to ensure each year group is able to follow the continuity and progression of skills to build upon each year. I have found the simplest way to do this is to take the 'Self-esteem strand', which has three main elements to cover. These are then divided into termly themes. Each year group covers termly:

Term One: Own capabilities

Term Two: Moods and feelings

Term Three: The big picture, How do I fit in?

Within each term there needs to be built in an equal distribution of skills, which link to self-esteem, communication, relationships and spiritual and moral development.

The A–Z lesson notes

The Circle Time lesson notes are written simply to ensure the lesson enables children to cover a range of activities, which are both fun and stimulating. Each lesson will have:

An introduction

This involves a round, energiser or game. You could begin with a positive thought to set the scene for the lesson. The introduction usually last 5–10 minutes.

The main feature

This is the main part of your lesson and should cover your learning outcome. This could be, for example, discussion, debate or a game, which involves problem solving activities or the use of the problem boxes. This usually lasts for 15–20 minutes.

Additional ideas

These are extra activities to support the Circle Time theme, they could be songs, activity or round.

To end your lesson

You may choose to end in a calming way with a dream journey, positive thought or you could also end in an energiser, such as a group yell or changing places game. You might wish to end in a song, or even a calming round.

At the finish of all lessons there may be a focus for the week on the Circle Time Notice Board. This may also involve parents.

There are examples at the end of this chapter of additional blank planning documents which can be used linked to the Citizenship Scheme of Work. All the lesson objectives are written at the top of the planner for ease of highlighting the appropriate strands of self-esteem, communication, relationships and spiritual and moral development. To go with the Key Stage One planning documents are the Citizenship objectives (p. 25), which can also be highlighted. If the planning document is linked to a unit of work in the Citizenship folder, you may wish to write the unit on the top of either planning document, e.g. Unit Two, Choices. In the Foundation Stage, the 'I Can' statements are at the top of the planning documents, as these are more appropriate.

Each lesson needs to have a main learning outcome, again on the reverse of the documents are examples of vocabulary to use to help you write these. This is then written at the top of the planning document.

Adaptations column

The adaptations column on the lesson planning document has been written to enable you to copy the document the following year and change elements of it slightly. It is to save you time! It is also to enable you to change your lesson, as appropriate to any developments before and during the lesson.

Headteachers and Ofsted Inspectors always like to see you have thought carefully about your planning and the annotated notes you write are often very useful to understanding how the lesson has evolved. You could also put further learning outcomes in this column, if you thought you needed further explanation of a specific section. It would be helpful to highlight the appropriate word, i.e. highlight 'adaptations' if that is how you have used the box and 'learning outcome' if you have written additional learning outcomes.

Resources required

Completing this column is vital to ensure you are well planned and you have all your resources to hand. A Circle Time resource box with a resource list on the top is always helpful. This could include:

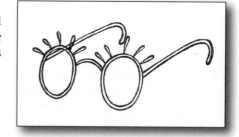

Resource box

- Parachute
- Glitter wig and wand
- Cuddly toys
- Hats x two
- Large ball
- Bubbles
- Puppets
- Pretend glasses and lashes

- Tambourine
- Ribbons
- Tapes
- String
- Coloured stickers
- Blindfold
- Bottle (for messages)
- Small box

Evaluation

Evaluations need only be short! We haven't got too much time to evaluate a fifteen to thirty minute lesson. Evaluations need to be to the point and explain if the lesson objectives have been achieved. They may also pinpoint groups of children who have achieved the lesson objectives or children who need additional help. They could also be used formatively to put forward ideas for the next lesson, e.g. must include co-operation skills next lesson.

Citizenship

It would be helpful to look at the QCA Citizenship folder (QCA ref – ISBN no: 1858384931) for the units of work and to use these to help plan your lesson. Further material which can be adapted to assist with this is the new SEAL curriculum, DCSF.

It should be emphasised that these blank lesson planning documents are to be used if you find them more helpful, for accountability purposes. They would certainly be helpful planning documents during Ofsted inspections. However, the lesson notes that have been planned in the A–Z Bear's Circle Time, can be used as working planning documents, space is given on the left hand side for your annotated notes or evaluations. It is your decision how effectively to use this planning section.

Suggested Strands of Circle Time Themes from Reception to Year Two

Self-esteem

- Own capabilities
- Moods and feelings
- The big picture – how do I belong/fit in?

Communication

- Speaking and listening
- Non-verbal
- Positive and negative communication.

Relationships

- Valuing and understanding others
- Good relationships
- Co-operation/fairness and justice
- Resolving conflict.

Spiritual and Moral Development

- Reflection and meditation
- Supporting each other and solving problems.

Citizenship Key Stage One Scheme of Work: Unit titles

Year	Unit no.	Unit title
1–2	1	Taking part – developing skills of communication and participation
1–2	2	Choices
1–2	3	Animals and us
1–2	4	People who help us – the police
1–2	5	Living in a diverse world
1–2	6	Developing our school grounds

All the strands noted on the previous pages can also be connected with the Excellence and Enjoyment documentation using the seven strands of:

1 Positive contribution
2 Be healthy
3 Creativity
4 Stay safe
5 Achievement
6 Responsible citizen
7 Well being.

One model of how Citizenship units can fit into termly schemes of work

		TERM One Own capabilities	TERM Two Moods and feelings	TERM Three The big picture – how do I belong/fit in?
Reception		U2 choices Likes/dislikes problem box, post person (Three terms)	U4 People who help us U6 Likes/dislikes in playground	Revisit Problem box, post person Problems and solutions
Year One		U2 Problem barrel Problems and Solutions (Three terms)	U6 Playground problems U2 Choices Likes/Dislikes Fair things/U2	U3 Animals and Us
Year Two		U2 choices What makes a good friend? U2 – problems Harry Potter – owl Problems and solutions (Three terms)	U4 People who help us U7 Children's rights	UI Developing skills of communication and participation

Other notes

Ensure there are termly problem boxes:

Unit 5 – Games, Living in a diverse world, to be covered in normal Circle Time activities.

Unit 8 – How do rules affect me? To be covered by all Units, linked to class codes.

Unit 11 – What's in the news? To be covered in Literacy lesson.

FOUNDATION STAGE: PERSONAL, SOCIAL AND HEALTH EDUCATION PLANNING SHEET

Early Learning goals

Personal, Social and Emotional development	Communication Language and Literacy	Creative Development	Other
I can cope with new experiences I can talk about experiences I have had at home I can behave appropriately I can express my needs and feelings I can take time and share fairly I can talk about my feelings in a positive way	I can sit and listen for 5 minutes I can participate in a small group I can describe with increasing clarity I can recall significant and less significant events I can interact with my peers questions and listen	I can join in with games and begin to respond to instructions I can use my body to build shapes I can work alone or with a partner I can talk about what I and others have done	I show an interest in new things I show care and concern for other people I can tell about people outside my family I understand the meaning of past and present I show sensitivity to other people's views, needs, cultures and beliefs
Introduction (Round, energiser, game)		Adaptations	Resources required
Main feature Round Discussion Problem solving/Puppet Bubble/Problem box		Adaptations	
Lesson ending Energiser, game, round, story, relaxation Pause for Thought/Song		Adaptations	Evaluation
Excellence and Enjoyment prompts:	Positive contribution Be healthy	Creativity Stay safe	Achievement Responsible citizens Well-being

KEY STAGE ONE: PERSONAL, SOCIAL AND HEALTH EDUCATION PLANNING SHEET

Lesson Objectives – *Please tick or highlight*

Self-esteem

To empower change.
To relate personal problems.
To be aware of physical capabilities.
To recognise ways to help self and others.
To recognise and respect we are all different and have individual values.
To recognise we all need support.
To feel confident about abilities.
To feel positive about self.

Relationships

To explore different emotions, feelings.
To be able to learn about friendships and caring.
To be able to deal positively with bullying behaviour.
To be able to understand fair play and treatment of others.
To be able to see how our actions affect others.

Spiritual and Moral

To use imagination to help us calm down and make sensible choices.
To understand the need for a quiet, reflective space.
To be reflective of self and others.

Communication

To explore through discussion.
To enable us to be aware and value other points of view.
To be able to describe.
To recognise ways to help.
To use a variety of games to explore moods and feelings.

Other

Main learning outcome (linked to main feature)/Links to Excellence and Enjoyment

Introduction (Round, energiser, game, positive thoughts)	**Adaptations/Learning Outcomes**
Main feature Round Discussion Problem solving/Puppet Bubble/Problem box. Problem solving game.	**Adaptations/Learning Outcomes**
Circle Time lesson ending Round/story/energiser/game/relaxation/dream journey/positive thoughts	**Adaptations/Learning Outcomes**

Resources required

Evaluation

LINKS TO CITIZENSHIP: KEY STAGE ONE

During Key Stage One, children learn about themselves as developing individuals and as members of their communities, building on their own experiences and on the early learning goals for personal, social and emotional development. The PSCHE and Citizenship guidelines include:

Developing confidence and responsibility and making the most of their abilities

1. Pupils should be taught:
   a. to recognise what they like and dislike, what is fair and unfair, and what is right and wrong.
   b. to share their opinions on things that matter to them and explain their views.
   c. to recognise, name and deal with their feelings in a positive way.

Preparing to play an active role as citizens

2. Pupils should be taught:
   a. to take part in discussions with one person and the whole class.
   b. to take part in a simple debate about topical issues.
   c. to recognise choices they can make, and recognise the difference between right and wrong.
   d. that they belong to various groups and communities, such as family and school.

Developing good relationships and respecting the differences between people

3. Pupils should be taught:
   a. to recognise how their behaviour affects other people.
   b. to listen to other people and play and work co-operatively.
   c. to identify and respect the differences and similarities between people.

Excellence and Enjoyment Prompt

- Positive contribution
- Be healthy
- Creativity
- Stay safe
- Achievement
- Responsible citizen
- Wellbeing

Learning outcome starters

Learn…
Know…
Emphasise…
Desirable…
Understand…
Recognise…
Are able to see…
Show that…
Reflect…
Use their skills…
Identify…
Demonstrate…
Think about…
Discuss…
Communicate…
Explain…

Lesson Objectives Linked to Strands of Self-esteem, Relationships, Communication and Spiritual and Moral Development

Adorable	To enable children to feel empowered to change things and situations around them.	Self-esteem
Bathtime	To enable children to relate personal problems anonymously. Discuss problems in a supportive way.	Self-esteem and relationships
Cool	To introduce relaxation by using a therapeutic story. To be able to understand the rules of the game.	Spiritual and moral development
Dancing	To explore the use of adjectives in playing games and group discussions.	Communication
Energetic	To develop the confidence to relate a descriptive story orally. To use imagination to develop ideas about cloud gazing.	Communication spiritual and moral development
Friendly	To explore the two different emotions of happy and sad. To recognise the qualities of friendship.	Relationships
Goalkeeper	To be aware of the physical capabilities of your body and to learn to overcome fears.	Self-esteem
Hiding	To confront worries and concerns and to empower children to discuss them in a safe environment.	Self-esteem and relationships
Ice-cream	To be able to describe favourite foods and to use senses to show enjoyment.	Communication
Jack-in-the-Box	To be able to use mime, discussion and drama to relate extreme feelings, e.g. Surprise and shock.	Self-esteem and communication
King	To recognise ways to help oneself and others.	Self-esteem and communication
Laughing	To explore happiness and sadness. To be able to deal with sad situations.	Self-esteem and relationships
Mending	To be able to learn how to retain friendships and how to be caring about one another.	Relationships
Noughts and Crosses	To be able to understand fair play and treatment of others.	Relationships
Orange Drinking	To explore the realms of space with our bodies and to join together with others in actions to create imaginative mime.	Communication and relationships
Party	To understand that we are all different and need support. To understand that some situations cause stress on individuals. To help us all enjoy leisure situations.	Self-esteem

Quiet Reading	To understand that we all need personal quiet space and to discuss ways of creating this.	Spiritual and moral development
Relaxing	To enable us to discover how to enjoy quality relaxation time.	Spiritual and moral development
Stripy	To understand that colours create moods and feelings and enhance telling stories.	Communication
Tall	To enable us to feel confident in our own abilities.	Self-esteem
Umbrella	To use a variety of games to explore working together as groups. To use dream journeys to create a feeling of calmness, fun and contentment.	Communication and Self-esteem
Very Happy	To understand how to deal with emotions of happiness and sadness. (followed up from Laughing bear)	Spiritual and moral development Self-esteem
WOW	To feel positive about self and others and to recognise each others strengths.	Self-esteem and relationships
Xylophone	To be able to recognise that others benefit from our help or need our kind thoughts.	Relationships
Yawning	To recognise that some of us are scared of the dark and need strategies to deal with this.	Spiritual and moral development
Zig Zag	To recognise that language does not need to be a barrier and that we communicate by feelings and expressions.	Communication

The table below shows which alphabetical word in the book is covered by which social strand. Included are Dream Journey, Positive Thought and Circle Time Notice Board.

Self-esteem	Communication	Relationships	Spiritual and Moral Development
Adorable (Dream journey)	Dancing (Notice board)	Bathtime	Cool (Dream journey/Positive thought)
Bathtime (Positive thought)	Energetic (Dream journey/ Notice board)	Friendly (Notice board)	Energetic (Dream journey/Notice board)
Goalkeeper (Dream journey)	Ice-Cream (Notice board)	Hiding (Positive thought)	Quiet Reading (Positive thought)
Hiding (Positive thought)	Jack-in-the-Box (Notice board)	Laughing (Positive thought)	Relaxing (Positive thought/Dream journey)
Jack-in-the-Box	King (Positive thought)	Mending (Positive thought)	Very happy (Positive thought)
King (Positive thought)	Orange Drinking (Notice board)	Noughts and crosses and Cool (Dream journey/ Positive thought)	Yawning (Positive thought)
Laughing (Positive thought)	Stripy (Positive thought)	Orange Drinking	Adorable and Hiding
Party (Notice board)	Umbrella (Positive thought)	WOW (Positive thought)	Ice-Cream and Jack-in-the-Box
Tall (Positive thought)	Cool	Xylophone (Positive thought)	King and Mending
Umbrella (Positive thought)			Party and Stripy
Very happy (Positive thought)			Tall and Umbrella
WOW (Positive thought)			WOW and Zig Zag (Notice board)

Introducing Creative Circle Time

This chapter gives you an example of a teachers script introducing both the bear and the alphabetical bear game to the class.

Example script

"Today we are going to begin our Circle Time sessions and to help us talk in our circle, I have brought along a very special friend. Our special friend is asleep, in this box in front of us, he is here to help us talk about lots of ideas and to help us learn how to make the right choices."

"In Circle Time we answer questions and talk together sitting in a circle. We are a friendship group who help each other solve problems. We pass ideas around the circle and we all try to speak, when it is out turn. We also play lots of games and have lots of fun."

"Let's see if we can wake up our bear. If we all whisper, 'Wake up, little bear,' I think he will wake up slowly and we can sit him in our circle of friends."

Children whisper, "Wake up, little bear," and the bear is taken out of the box by the teacher and is placed on her lap.

"In our Circle Time sessions we pass the bear around the circle. When he is sitting on your knee, it is your turn to speak. Let's just pass him around the circle and introduce yourself to him. You can say, 'My name is ....., good morning little bear'."

Bear is passed around the circle and each child speaks and the final one to speak is the teacher.

"Let me remind you of the rules of Circle Time. In Circle Time:

- We listen to each other
- We may say 'pass' if we cannot think of something to say
- We do not put each other down. This means we do not say anything which is unkind about each other
- We do not tell anybody what they should be doing
- When we try to help each other we say, 'Do you think it would be helpful if...?'
- We behave well and tell the truth
- And finally, we speak when our special bear is sitting on our knee, or by raising our hand, like this." (Teacher demonstrates).

"Now let's have a look at our special alphabet posters and learn about our other special bears. These posters will be put around our room to help us with our alphabet. There is also a poem or a song to learn for each letter of the alphabet."

Teacher reads through A-Z of alphabet posters and shows them the pictures of each bear.

"We are now going to try and play the first part of our Alphabetical game."

See Alphabetical game – Challenge one.

At the end of Alphabetical game:

"At the beginning of each lesson we will be introduced to bears with different names. But which name should we give to our special bear? His name needs to begin with a 'B', because all the bears in the book begin with a 'B'."

"Let's try and find a special name for our bear. Also children, it has to have two syllables – let me tap you two syllables like in the names Bran-don, Brind-ley."

Teacher taps two syllables

"Let's see if we can choose a name..."

"Have we any suggestions...?"

Alphabetical bear game

This game needs to be played after the children have had a number of sessions going through the alphabetical bear order and also being introduced to their bear.

Rules of the alphabet game

Give each child a strip of alphabetical words, e.g. **B** is for **B**athtime bear, **F** is for **F**riendly bear. The children can then be set the first challenge:

Alphabetical challenge one
They need to make three alphabetical lines in order.

They are allowed to talk and help each other.

Show the children where to form the lines by alphabetical cards on the floor.

The cards should say:

Line One	A–I
Line Two	J–R
Line Three	S–Z

At the end of the challenge the children have to call out their alphabetical bear card to see if they have managed the correct order. If they are not in order, the other two lines are allowed to help them.

A clap is always given for effort and then the cards are returned to the teacher, where they will be redistributed for the next game (this could be the next lesson).

Alphabetical challenge two
Is the same as challenge one, but this time the children have to get into alphabetical order without talking. They may point, mime, show each other their cards, but not lip read. This is a much harder and quite an amusing challenge to observe.

Alphabetical challenge three
This game can then be made more challenging by forming two lines, A–M and N–Z.

Use challenge one first of talking and then challenge two of not talking.

Alphabetical challenge four
The final challenge is to use both methods to form the line A–Z.

This game is great fun and the children really enjoy this challenge.

The success is well rewarded by a round of applause and personal pat on the back.

A is for adorable bear

B is for bathtime bear

C is for cool bear

D is for dancing bear

E is for energetic bear

F is for friendly bear

G is for goalkeeper
bear

H is for hiding
bear

I is for ice-cream
bear

J   is for Jack-in-the-box bear

K   is for king bear

L   is for laughing bear

M is for mending bear

N is for noughts and crosses bear

O is for orange drinking bear

P is for party bear

Q is for quiet reading bear

R is for relaxing bear

S is for stripy bear

T is for tall bear

U is for umbrella bear

V is for very happy bear

W is for WOW bear

X is for xylophone bear

Y is for yawning bear

Z is for zig zag bear

Y

Y is for yawning
bear

Z

Z is for zig zag
bear

Lesson Plans A–Z

Icons used in Lesson plans to indicate the different
components of Circle Time

Round

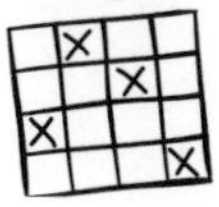

Game

Musical Activity

Discussion/Group

Bear puppet/Problem Solving

Bubble Time

Energiser

Dream Journey

Positive Thought

Story

Class Circle Time Notice Board

Adorable

Lesson objective: To enable children to feel empowered to change things and situations around them.

Citizenship: Children to share their opinions about things that matter.

Introduction: Read poem and perform poem to rhythm (this either to be done before the Circle Time lesson in literacy lesson or at the beginning of Circle Time session).

Adorable bear

Adorable bear, hiding in a yellow tree,
Send me a smile, addressed to me,
Post it and seal it, in an envelope blue,
And I'll send you one back, just for you.

Adorable bear, you look golden and bright,
The yellow glows around you, an incredible sight,
Send me a wish, a wish I can hold,
Adorable bear, you've a heart of gold.

Preparation for the lesson/Resources   Audio track – Adorable bear

Resources: Bear.

(CD of rhythms needed for every lesson and box of instruments). Parachute.

Two different coloured hats for old hat, new hat (one looking older and, one newer).

INTRODUCTION Energiser, in circle, changing places	*Introduction, Reminder Circle Time Rules* **Food we adore** All those who adore chips…change places. All those who adore… pizza, curry, crisps, chocolate, etc. **Places we adore** All those who adore going to: the pictures, McDonald's, holidays, etc., change places. (This can also be done under a parachute!)
MAIN FEATURE 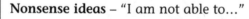	Two different coloured hats. Children put first hat on and say: "I used to be able to…" (in the past). Change to second hat – "But now I am able to…" (in the present). e.g. "I used to be able to crawl and now I am able to walk." Pass this idea all the way round the circle. "I would like to be able to…" (in the future). Teacher may wish to have an open discussion on how they would achieve some of their 'future ideas'. How can they 'change' things for a better future? **Nonsense ideas** – "I am not able to…" (e.g. Stand on my head in a bucket of water while riding my bicycle).
LESSON ENDING **ADDITIONAL IDEAS**	First quietly and then louder. (All children may wish to tap their knees to build up crescendo). Begin Ah…Ah…Ah… and, as the crescendo builds up, the teacher gives a sign and then all jump up and shout ADORABLE.

Introducing dream journeys

To begin introducing dream journeys allocate a separate lesson dedicated to the techniques and allow the children time to practise these. Let the children concentrate on breathing, movement and relaxation techniques used at the beginning and end of each dream journey. Once these are accomplished, dream journeys can be incorporated into Circle Time lessons.

Dream journey

Say to the children, "Breathe in slowly and out slowly. Remember to keep your eyes closed and just listen to your breathing. Now wriggle your fingers, then relax them and let them be still. Now move your head slowly from side to side and now relax it and be still. Well done! Now we are ready to listen to our story."

Imagine you are able to go to your favourite place. It could be your grandparents' house, a favourite garden or park. It could be a favourite holiday or even somewhere special in your house. Imagine yourself there, think carefully about what favourite things you would like to do there. In your mind, see yourself sitting, lying or walking in your favourite place. Focus on what you actually see and feel, especially think about what you see close around you. You feel really happy, this is your special place and no-one can take it away from you.

Hold on to your thoughts and think about all those special things you can do.

You **adore** this place.

It is so special, enjoy yourself and enjoy feeling special.

(Give approximately three minutes for the children to think to themselves).

At the end of the dream journey, remind the children to breathe slowly and listen to their own quiet breathing. Tell them, "Breathe in and out slowly and feel relaxed. Now wriggle your fingers then relax them and let them be still. Now move your head slowly from side to side and now relax it and be still. When you are ready, open your eyes. Well done everyone. You listened really well."

Allow for quiet reflection before moving on to the feedback stage.

Questions

* Which favourite place did you go to?
* What could you see?
* Using your other senses. What could you taste, smell, touch and hear?
* How did you feel about being there?
* Why did it make you feel really happy?
* What else makes you feel happy and special?

This is a model for all dream journeys, where questions are asked appropriate to the journey the children have taken, during the quiet reflection time.

Bathtime

Lesson objective: To enable children to relate personal problems anonymously. To discuss problems in a supportive way.

Citizenship: To recognise, identify and deal with their feelings in a positive way.

Introduction: Read poem and perform poem to rhythm (this either to be done before the Circle Time lesson in Literacy lesson or at the beginning of Circle Time session).

Baloo bathtime bear

Baloo, Baloo, a bathtime bear,
Bubbles and soap everywhere.

Washing his front, scrubbing his toes,
Bathtime bubbles all over his nose.

Playing at crocodiles, hands open wide,
Let all the fishes swim inside.

Jaws goes snip, Jaws goes snap,
Water's getting cold, turn on hot tap.

Water's getting hot, on his toes,
Pull the plug out, down it goes.

Baloo, Baloo, a bathtime bear,
Bubbles and soap everywhere.

Preparation for the lesson/Resources   Audio track – Bathtime bear

Preparation:	Need to prepare a bubble burst problem box, for children to put messages in (see Chapter 4). Also prepare bubble popper (similar to magic wand). Song, "I'm forever blowing bubbles."
Resources:	Bear. Two sets of bubbles. Tambourine.
Circle Time Notice Board: (information on CD)	See Chapter 2 for preparation of Circle Time notice board.
Positive Thought Script:	✓

INTRODUCTION 	Take some bubbles into the lesson and blow them in front of the children. Ask the children to look at them really carefully and ask for descriptive words about the bubbles. Make a list of all the describing words. Ask the children to turn to a partner and to complete the sentence. "If I could float and be as light as a bubble I would…" Send the bubbles around the circle. Let each child blow a bubble and say, "If I could float and be as light as a bubble I would…"

MAIN FEATURE
 	
	Problem box, Chapter 4
	Introduce to the children, 'bubble burst' problem box.
	
	The children can either write a note or a message and post it in the problem box and the group can then help each other with it at bubble burst (Circle Time). Tell the children at bubble burst we pass bubbles around to blow our cares away. The bubbles help us feel relaxed.
	
	Also, introduce them to a bear who can be there to help with problems. If children think they can help with a problem, they can talk through the bear and say, "Would it help if…"
	
	Also, the teacher may use the bear to help with problems.
	
	All problems are anonymous so the children don't know who has written them. If there is a serious problem, the child can put their name in the box on a bubble
	
	e.g. Mrs Weatherhead,
	        I need to talk
	        to you – Claire.
	
	The teacher will then find a private time to see that child.
	
	Bubble burst needs to be introduced in a supportive, calm and relaxed way.
	
	The teacher may also put in 'known problems'.

ADDITIONAL IDEAS Sing	Sing, "I'm forever blowing bubbles."

LESSON ENDING

Children all join hands in a circle and stand up.

They pretend they are one large bubble and they can stretch and shrink and make the bubble into as many different shapes as they can. Teacher to use tambourine to shout out bubble instructions.

e.g. stretch, shrink, thin, fat, spiky, etc.

The teacher then introduces the children to a 'bubble popper stick'.

The teacher tells the children when she pops the large bubble, each child becomes a separate bubble and they can move about changing shape, shouting pop, pop or pp…pop.

When the teacher shouts BUBBLE, they all join together again and the process begins again.

Introducing the Circle Time Notice Board

Teacher's script:

"We have made a special Circle Time Notice Board. This is your own board to add your own positive thoughts or ideas to. These may be drawings, paintings, writing, a collection of papers or objects. This board belongs to our Circle Time group."

The notice board then becomes a feature for the week of anything the children wish to put on it, connected with the theme for the week. It is referred to at various times throughout the week.

Parents are also encouraged to contribute ideas to this.

Positive thought for the week

Feel special this week.

Write down on our special paper, something that makes you feel special.

Place it on our Circle Time Notice Board.

Cool

Lesson objective: To introduce relaxation by using a therapeutic story.
To be able to understand the rules of games.

Citizenship: To listen to other people and play and work co-operatively.

Introduction: Read poem and perform poem to rhythm (this either to be done before the Circle Time lesson in Literacy lesson or at the beginning of Circle Time session).

Cool bear

Only an ice cool bear
Could really share,
The pond with the goldfish ten.

Only an ice cool bear
Could really dare,
To dip his toes in the cool fountain.

Only an ice cool bear
Could sunbathe there,
In the pool that ripples with rings.

Only an ice cool bear
Could dreamily stare,
At the butterflies with colourful wings.

Preparation for the lesson/Resources   Audio track – Cool bear

Preparation: Prepare fish shape (child hand size).

Resources: Bear.

                        Real ice cube.

Positive Thought Script: ✓

INTRODUCTION

Pass on the word fish with a wiggle of the hand.

Emphasise the '**sh**' at the end of fi**sh-sh**

MAIN FEATURE

Send a child out of the room. One child is given a 'cool fish' to sit on.

(Cut out fish shape)

The child returns and is allowed to ask three children a question.
e.g. "Am I warm in finding the cool fish?"

If the child who is asked the question, has the fish, they have to show it and then they go out of the room themselves. The process begins again.

If they are sitting **next to** someone who has the fish, they have to answer, "The fish are frying. They are so hot." If they are **near to** someone they reply, "You are very warm." If they are nowhere near, the child replies, "You're a cold fish."

After three guesses the child goes to the centre of the circle and chooses where to count the word FISH from.

They count round four children **F I S H** and ask the last child

"Am I warm in finding the cool fish?"

(Same rules for reply as above).

If the fish is not found, it is then revealed and the child with the fish is 'on'.

Repeat the process.

ADDITIONAL IDEAS

Pass on a smile.

A wink.

Pass on a real ice cube and say 'cool ice'.

LESSON ENDING

Say to the children, "Breathe in slowly and out slowly. Remember to keep your eyes closed and just listen to your breathing. Now wriggle your fingers, then relax them and let them be still. Now move your head slowly from side to side and now relax it and be still. Well done! Now we are ready to listen to our story."

Imagine you are a cool bear and you are lying sunbathing by the pond on a lovely sunny day.

You really think you are a 'real cool bear'... you have your 'cool' sunglasses on and you lie there listening to the sound of the fountain, splashing cooling water into the pond. You dream really happy thoughts. Feel the sun's rays on your face and feel that warm tingling feeling inside. You feel relaxed, carefree and contented.

Lie there for a few minutes and continue your happy relaxing dreams... Make it a special moment.

At the end of the dream journey, remind the children to breathe slowly and listen to their own quiet breathing. Tell them, "Breathe in and out slowly and feel relaxed. Now wriggle your fingers then relax them and let them be still. Now move your head slowly from side to side and now relax it and be still. When you are ready, open your eyes. Well done everyone. You listened really well."

Allow for quiet reflection before moving on to the next stage.

Questions

- Which happy thoughts did you dream?
- How did you feel with the warm sun on your face?
- Why do you think you look 'cool' in sunglasses? What does it mean to be 'cool'?
- What do you do to help you relax?

Positive thought for the week

Feel *relaxed* this week.

Draw a picture of you being relaxed.

What are you doing?
Where are you?
How do you feel?

Place it on our Circle Time Notice Board.

Dancing

Lesson objective: To explore the use of adjectives in playing games and group discussions.

Citizenship: To recognise what children like and dislike.

Introduction: Read poem and perform poem to rhythm (this either to be done before the Circle Time lesson in Literacy lesson or at the beginning of Circle Time session).

Dancing bear

Barney, Barney, is a dancing bear,
He loves to rock and roll.

And when he's out a partying,
He is the life and soul.

He's got good rhythm, he's really smooth,
He likes to dance, he loves to groove.

He finds a friend, they dance all night,
They leap about, a brilliant sight.

He loves his friend, to throw him high,
He stretches up, into the sky.

He lands on the ground, in the splits he goes,
And then quick as a flash, on to his toes.

Barney, Barney, is a dancing bear,
He loves to rock and roll.

And when he's out a partying,
He is the life and soul!

Preparation for the lesson/Resources   Audio track – Dancing bear

Preparation: CD and any lively music.

Resources: Bear.

                              Paper or card for writing pop groups on.

Circle Time Notice Board Poster: ✓

INTRODUCTION

Begin by standing in a circle and dancing to some music, freeze when the music stops.

Copy a rhythm to a piece of music. Sustain the rhythm and change it.

MAIN FEATURE

Make a list of favourite pop groups, e.g. Boyzone, Travis, Robbie Williams.

Use the names to make an alliterative sentence. (i.e. *Boyzone* are *brilliant*).

e.g.   Boyzone are brilliant.
          Travis are terrific.
          Robbie Williams is WOW.

Ask the children to think of as many different adjectives as they can collect, which begin with the same letter as their groups.

Choose three Pop Stars and the children repeat their names in a round style, similar to repeating three objects.

e.g.   Child One – Boyzone; Child Two – Travis; Child Three – Robbie;
          Child Four – Boyzone; Child Five – Travis; Child Six – Robbie, etc.

Once the children have a named pop star to remember, go round the circle again and ask them to choose a describing word that begins with the same letter, about their pop star e.g. Bizarre Boyzone, Tremendous Travis, Raging Robbie.

Teacher then introduces three instructions, HIGH, LOW, NODDING.
If the child's Pop Star is called out, they have to swap places in the manner that it is called out.

e.g.   Boyzone swap places nodding, the instruction would be Nodding Boyzone.
          High Travis – children stretch high and swap places.
          Low Robbie – children crawl.

ADDITIONAL IDEAS

Partners

Children are asked to imagine they are at a disco.

They need to think of their favourite clothes that they would like to wear for this disco.

Turning to a partner, they need to describe these clothes, including their shoes.

They need to ensure they have a describing word (adjective) for each article of clothing.

e.g.   green T-shirt.
          sparkling shoes.
          stripy dress.

Children choose one article of clothing they have described from the above and share it in round form.

e.g.   Child One – Sparkly shoes; Child Two – Red T-shirt;
         Child Three – Green shorts.

LESSON ENDING

After the round has finished the teacher tells the children they are to connect with at least two other children to make up a disco outfit.

    Child One   Child Two   Child Three

e.g. sparkling shoes, red T-shirt, black trousers.

The teacher counts down 10, 9, 8… 0 and then asks the children to stand in their clothes groups before the count of 0.

When the groups have made their outfits, they describe it to the rest of the group.

They explain why they like this outfit.

Circle Time Notice Board

Draw or bring in a photograph of yourself
wearing your favourite 'dancing' or 'party' clothes.

Energetic

Lesson objective: To develop the confidence to relate a descriptive story orally.
To use imagination to develop ideas about cloud gazing.

Citizenship: To take part in discussion with the whole class.

Introduction: Read poem and perform poem to rhythm (this either to be done before the Circle Time lesson in Literacy lesson or at the beginning of Circle Time session).

Energetic bear

Do you dare, do you dare,
Stand on your head like energetic bear?

Upside down, Upside down,
The world is as funny as a circus clown.

Count to ten, wriggle your toes,
Do it one-handed and hold your nose.

Do you dare, do you dare,
Stand on your head like energetic bear?

Preparation for the lesson/Resources

Audio track – Energetic bear

Resources:
- Bear
- Whistle or bell
- Problem box
- Bubbles

Circle Time Notice Board Poster: ✓

INTRODUCTION	"When I grow up I want to be…" "My favourite game in the playground is…"

MAIN FEATURE Pairs
 	
 Instructions
	Ask the children to pretend they are a postman or woman.
	
	In pairs, one child begins to talk through their journey as they deliver the letters.
	
	Describe what you pass, e.g. shops, houses, gardens, parks, etc. and also which people you meet.
	
	Teacher has a whistle or a bell. Every time the whistle is blown, the other child continues describing the journey.
	
	Now introduce describing words and energy words to describe people. The children have to use adjectives to describe their journey.
	
	Tell them the rules now are that in every sentence they must say:
	
	    One thing they **saw**.
	    One thing they **passed**.
	    And a person with an **action**.
	
	Have cards to remind them: SAW – PASSED – ACTION.
	
	e.g. I saw a **blue** front door and I passed a **jagged** fence and I saw Mr Brown who was **jogging**.
	
	Volunteer some children to demonstrate.

ADDITIONAL IDEAS 	Discuss any bubble problems from the bubble burst box. Use the bear to help solve problems.

LESSON ENDING

Tell the children they have just been doing something really energetic like dancing, riding a bike, swimming or playing tig.

Say to the children, "Breathe in slowly and out slowly. Remember to keep your eyes closed and just listen to your breathing. Now wriggle your fingers, then relax them and let them be still. Now move your head slowly from side to side and now relax it and be still. Well done! Now we are ready to listen to our story."

Try and imagine a clear blue sky with white fluffy clouds floating across the blue.

As you watch the clouds they change into different shapes, see how many different shapes you can make from the clouds.

Can you make:

  a fairy castle
  a galloping horse
  a slithering snake
  a white daisy
  a ferocious monster

Now try and think up your own shapes and lie and relax, breathing really slowly. Your body should feel light and carefree.

(Give the children time to think).

At the end of the dream journey, remind the children to breathe slowly and listen to their own quiet breathing. Tell them, "Breathe in and out slowly and feel relaxed. Now wriggle your fingers then relax them and let them be still. Now move your head slowly from side to side and now relax it and be still. When you are ready, open your eyes. Well done everyone. You listened really well."

Allow for quiet reflection before moving on to the next stage.

Questions

• Which shapes did you make with the clouds?
• Did you see any scary shapes?
• Did you make any unusual shapes?
• How did you feel when you were cloud gazing?

Circle Time Notice Board

Be a 'cloud gazer' this week

Draw the shapes you see.

Put them on our Circle Time Notice Board.

Can you write any stories about the shapes you saw?

Friendly

Lesson objective: To explore the two different emotions of happy and sad.
                     To recognise the qualities of friendship.

Citizenship: To recognise and deal with their feelings in a positive way.

Introduction: Read poem and perform poem to rhythm (this either to be done before the Circle Time lesson in Literacy lesson or at the beginning of Circle Time session).

Friendly bear

If you need a friend,
To share all your news,
Bradley will be that friend,
He's the one to choose.
He's a friend in a million,
He will love you and care,
And when you feel sad,
Bradley will always be there.
To listen to your troubles,
To put round you his arm,
And with Bradley near you,
You will come to no harm.

63

Preparation for the lesson/Resources   Audio track – Friendly bear

Preparation:	A box of instruments, one per child, e.g. tambourine, hand drum, shakers, sticks, etc.
Resources:	Bear.
	Paper and pens.
	Bubbles.
Circle Time Notice Board Poster:	✓

INTRODUCTION

Pass the bear round the circle and say…

"We need friends because…"

"We should help each other because…"

Make a group list of all the qualities of a true friend.

MAIN FEATURE

 Partners

In partners, tell each other about your friend. Describe their qualities and explain exactly why you like them.

Don't mention their name.

Share some ideas with the circle.

ADDITIONAL IDEAS

Children alternatively go round the circle using expressions and mime to help Happy, Sad, Happy, Sad.

Pass bubbles around the circle.

Children say, "I am sad when…" and blow a bubble following this.

Put the bear in the middle of the circle.

Teacher or children can offer to help others by using the bear and saying:

"Would it help when you're sad if…?"

LESSON ENDING

HAPPY!

Children stand up…tapping or shaking instruments quietly and saying happy. Build up to a crescendo and, on teacher's instruction, JUMP UP, ARMS OUTSTRETCHED AND SHOUT HAPPY!

Circle Time Notice Board

For our Circle Time Notice Board draw or bring in a picture, or write about what makes you happy.

Our title will be:
"I am happy when..."

Goalkeeper

Lesson objective: To be aware of the physical capabilities of your body and to learn to overcome fears.

Citizenship: To recognise and respect the similarities and differences between people.

Introduction: Sing Song (this either to be done before the Circle Time lesson in Literacy lesson or at the beginning of Circle Time session).

Goalkeeper bear (with music)
(Try and put in actions to song!)

Dribble the ball,
Kick the ball,
Aim it at the goal.
Dive for the ball,
Leap for the ball,
Do a forward roll.

Preparation for the lesson/Resources   Audio track – Goalkeeper bear

Preparation: Action cards, e.g. digging, washing, brushing teeth, washing hair, cleaning a car, etc.

Resources: Puppet, Bear.

Ball (football size).

Circle Time Notice Board Poster: ✓

INTRODUCTION

Sing Goalkeeper bear.

MAIN FEATURE

Begin a round. Name something physical you find a difficulty in doing.

e.g. Riding a bike, climbing a rope, swimming, etc. (share some ideas).

Teacher may stop the round or ask children to help other children through the use of a puppet.

Then say: "Would it help if…"

e.g. "I find it difficult to ride a bike."

Child or Teacher: "Would it help if you had stabilisers on?"
                       "Would it help if you practised with a friend?"

In a round: Name as many action words as you can think of,

e.g. run, skip, jump, throw, hop, swim, climb, etc.

Have a go in pairs miming action words for your partner to guess.

Use pre-prepared actions on cards.

e.g. digging, washing, brushing teeth, washing hair, cleaning a car.

ADDITIONAL IDEAS

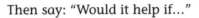

Whilst rolling a ball to each other across the circle, name anything you can do with a ball.

e.g. bounce it, throw it, sit on it, kick it, blow it up, shoot with it, score with it, pass it, etc.

LESSON ENDING

Say to the children, "Breathe in slowly and out slowly. Remember to keep your eyes closed and just listen to your breathing. Now wriggle your fingers, then relax them and let them be still. Now move your head slowly from side to side and now relax it and be still. Well done! Now we are ready to listen to our story."

You pretend that air is flowing through your legs, making them feel light and fresh. You wriggle your toes to help them relax. The air passes through your feet and up through your legs very slowly.

Now you concentrate on your breathing, breathe slowly in and then out. This time try to hold your breath to the count of 4 seconds.

Breathe slowly in – 1, 2, 3, 4 and out – 1, 2, 3, 4.
Again, in – 1, 2, 3, 4 and out – 1, 2, 3, 4.

Now let's concentrate on your heart. Think of a place you really love to be at. Is it the park? Your garden? Your bedroom? Your Grandma's house? Pretend you are there, happy and relaxed. Hold that thought for a few minutes and think about that place and how happy you feel.

Give the children time to think.

At the end of the dream journey, remind the children to breathe slowly and listen to their own quiet breathing. Tell them, "Breathe in and out slowly and feel relaxed. Now wriggle your fingers then relax them and let them be still. Now move your head slowly from side to side and now relax it and be still. When you are ready, open your eyes. Well done everyone. You listened really well."

Allow for quiet reflection before moving on to the next stage.

Circle Time Notice Board

Bring in pictures, photographs or drawings of your favourite sport.

It could be yourself involved in this sport, or it could be your favourite sporting star.

Our sentence this week to complete is:

Exercise is good because…

HIDING

Lesson objective: To confront worries and concerns and to empower children to discuss them in a safe environment.

Citizenship: To share opinions on things that matter to them and explain their views.

Introduction: Read poem and perform poem to rhythm (this either to be done before the Circle Time lesson in Literacy lesson or at the beginning of Circle Time session).

Hiding bear

Let's play hide and seek, run and hide!
Bronty will be "on" and we'll run inside,
We'll hide behind curtains, hide in the bath,
And if Bronty finds us, he'll probably laugh,
We'll hide under tables, we'll hide behind chairs,
We'll hide behind the fridge and under the stairs,
Let's play hide and seek, run and hide,
Bronty will be "on" and we'll run inside.

Preparation for the lesson/Resources	**Audio track – Hiding bear**

Preparation:	Small treasure for hiding (e.g. a sparkling bead, a pretend jewel, a gold coin).
Resources:	Bear.
	Bubbles.
	Problem box.
Positive Thought Script:	✓

INTRODUCTION	Hidden treasure
	
	Ask one child to go out of the room.
	
	Hide some treasure on one child.
	
	The child who returns is able to ask three children questions about the location of the treasure.
	
	Questions may include:
	
	    Question One: Is it with a boy or girl?
	    Question Two: Am I close or far away?
	    Question Three: Is it Paul? Is it Gail? Is it Rehana?
	
	After the third question, the child needs to guess the location of the treasure, if they haven't already found it.
	
	If the child is correct, they choose someone else to go out to guess and the treasure is moved. If the child is incorrect, the child hiding the treasure goes out.

MAIN FEATURE	Send the bubbles around the circle and tell the children they are going to put their worries inside the bubbles and blow them away. As the bubbles pop, so will their worries disappear. The first round is a silent round, where bubbles are blown high and children think about a worry they have – that they can blow away. (Usually two sets of bubbles are useful). Teacher then discusses any bubble worries, put in the bubble burst box. Children are reminded that some bubble worries may need to be discussed individually with the teacher, as some may need extra help from the teacher as worries will not go away immediately.
ADDITIONAL IDEAS 	"My favourite place to think is…" "I feel I would like to hide from people when…" Use the bear to try and help some individual bubble problems. Teacher and children. "Would it help if…"
LESSON ENDING Energiser	Pass a pretend bubble around the circle. Don't pop it! After it has been passed around – after the numbers 1, 2, 3 – everyone shout POP! and clap hands.

Positive thought for the week

Think about something that
makes you smile.

Draw a picture, bring in a photograph or write
about something that makes
you smile.

Make some smiley faces badges.

Stick them on our Circle Time Notice Board.

Ice-cream

Lesson objective: To be able to describe favourite foods and to use senses to show enjoyment.

Citizenship: To take part in discussions.

Introduction: Read poem and perform poem to rhythm (this either to be done before the Circle Time lesson in Literacy lesson or at the beginning of Circle Time session).

Ice-cream bear

Scrumptious, delicious, ice-cream in a dollop,
A super duper mouthful, what a wallop,
Icy in the mouth, shivery down your throat,
Icy-wicy, dicey, crikey, it's like an ice cream boat,
Sailing down the tunnels, that are
dark and scary inside,
Sliding fast towards your stomach,
It's a very bumpy ride,
Scrumptious, delicious ice-cream in a dollop
Arriving in your stomach, what an icy wallop!

Preparation for the lesson/Resources   Audio track – Ice-cream bear

Resources: Bear.

                              Parachute.

Circle Time Notice Board Poster: ✓

INTRODUCTION

"My favourite ice-cream is…"

Choose child in the middle of circle.

Child says: "Anyone who likes chocolate ice-cream, change places."
            "Anyone who likes chocolate chip ice-cream, change places."
            "Anyone who likes a flake in their ice-cream, change places."

This can also be a changing place game under a parachute.

A word to describe my favourite ice cream is …

MAIN FEATURE

Discuss with your friend your favourite dessert.

Say why you like it and when you are normally able to eat it.

Choose one dessert describing word to show how much you like it. e.g. Creamy yogurts, mouth watering melons, delicious ice-cream.

Now return to the circle and each partner describes their friend's favourite dessert, including using the describing word.

ADDITIONAL IDEAS

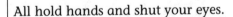

Look at the bubble burst problem box, or ask the children if they have any problems to bring to bubble burst.

Use the bear to help solve problems.

"Would it help if…"

LESSON ENDING

All hold hands and shut your eyes.

After the count of three … say the word SHIVER and send a group SHIVER across the circle.

Keep holding hands and say the word ICY and send an ICY SHIVER around the circle.

Now send the word TINGLING and WARM round the circle and children end in a group hug.

Circle Time Notice Board

**Do you deserve to treat
yourself this week?**

See if you can have a favourite food this week.
Make sure you are good so you deserve
this treat.

Bring in a wrapper, container
or drawing of your
favourite food.

Place it on our
Circle Time Notice Board.

Delicious!

Jack-in-the-box

Lesson objective: To be able to use mime, discussion and drama to relate extreme feelings, e.g. Surprise and shock.

Citizenship: To recognise what they like and dislike.

Introduction: Read poem and perform poem to rhythm (this either to be done before the Circle Time lesson in Literacy lesson or at the beginning of Circle Time session).

Jack-in-the-box bear

Brindle's become a Jack-in-the-box,
He jumps and springs, SURPRISE!
He loves to be a secret toy,
Who leaps up and waves goodbye.

Preparation for the lesson/Resources

Audio track – Jack in the box bear

Preparation: Individual letters on cards to make the word SURPRISE:

[S] [U] [R] [P] [R] [I] [S] [E]

Any music you can mime opening a parcel to.

Resources: Bear.

Tambourine.

Circle Time Notice Board Poster: ✓

INTRODUCTION	Group Yell – SURPRISE! Children to start low, like a Jack-in-the-box and, after the count of three, jump up, using arms stretched out and shout SURPRISE! Do this like a Mexican wave, round the circle, one child at a time.
MAIN FEATURE	"The best surprise I ever had was…" "I would like to surprise my mum, dad, brother, sister, friend by…" "The worst shock I ever had was…" Have four sets of the word SURPRISE made on individual letter cards, e.g. one set [S] [U] [R] [P] [R] [I] [S] [E]. Eight children could then spell the word, each with an individual letter. Give out as many sets of individual letters as you can, i.e. three lots of eight letters will be for twenty four children. Four lots of eight letters for thirty two children. (Some children may need to watch the game the first time if there are uneven numbers). Children then need to be told they are going to try and make as many full words of SURPRISE as they can. Remind the children how to spell the word SURPRISE. The children then need to stand up and try and find clusters of letters and stand in a line in the correct letter order to spell the word SURPRISE by holding their letters up and forming the word. Put the children in groups of four. Tell the children they have ten seconds (countdown 10, 9, 8…) to get in a freeze frame that looks SURPRISED. Use tambourine to indicate ready to look at freeze frame, i.e. 10, 9, 8, 7, 6, 5, 4, 3, 2, 1 (tambourine noise). Now change the freeze frame to a: • Jack-in-the-Box • Scarecrow • Spring • Puppet on a string • Letter 'J' • SURPRISE parcel.

| **LESSON ENDING**

 | To Music (Mime)

Read out script below, slowly to any chosen slow music.

"Now imagine you have a Surprise parcel in front of you.

The shape is really exciting and you look at it, trying to decide what it is. It is tied up with a ribbon and you decide to slowly pull the ribbon away from the parcel. Now start to open the sellotape and begin to unwrap the wrapping paper.

Pull it off slowly and, as the last layer comes off, you are utterly SURPRISED.

Show your surprise and freeze."

"In my Surprise parcel was…" |

Circle Time Notice Board

Can you draw or write about your favourite
surprise?

Or have you got a photograph of it?

Place it on our Circle Time Notice Board.

Share it with us all.

King

Lesson objective: To recognise ways to help oneself and others.

Citizenship: To recognise choices they can make.

Introduction: Read poem (this poem does not have a rhythm – it is to be read majestically) this either to be done before the Circle Time lesson in Literacy lesson or at the beginning of Circle Time session.

King bear

Your majesty Bazal, can I have a little word?
I've a secret for to tell, and it's really so absurd,
I had a dream last night, I dreamt the world turned white,
I dreamt that all our school, lost its colour over night,
The crayons had no colours, unless we coloured snow,
The paints they were just white, the rainbows had to go,
The children's songs were boring, no colours we could sing,
The displays around the corridors, had turned to ghostly scenes,
The teachers all wore white, they looked so ill and drawn,
They didn't know what to teach, they really looked forlorn,
But one day in Assembly, the headteacher shed a tear,
She tried to talk of Spring, no colours would appear.
The tear fell on you Sire, on your rainbow colours bright,
And your colours made a stream, it was such a wonderful sight,
And as if a magic rainbow, had come to save us all,
The colours touched the displays and made a brilliant coloured hall,
The children found their smiles, they sang with life and zest,
The teachers looked delighted, they said we really did our best,
Your Majesty you see, your colours mean life is worth living,
We thank you for our colours, and for the joy that you are giving.

Preparation for the lesson/Resources   Audio track – King bear

Preparation:	Question cards – Who? How? What? Words for 'Grand Old Duke of York' (and music if possible).
Resources:	Bear. Problem box. Bubbles.
Positive Thought Script:	✓

INTRODUCTION

"If I were a king I would…"

"If I could grant three wishes they would be…"

MAIN FEATURE

Pairs

Discuss in pairs who you would help if you were able to.

How would you go about trying to help them?

What would be the end results you would hope for?

Questions to consider, Who? How? What?

Share some of the ideas with the whole of the group

"I wish I could be better at…"

Stop at various points and ask the children to help, using the bear.

"Would it help if…"

ADDITIONAL IDEAS

Bubble burst, discuss any problems from the box.

Use bear to help.

LESSON ENDING

Stand Up

- Sing 'The Grand Old Duke of York' and march standing up
- Second time, miss out singing 'UP', just put hand up in air
- Third time, miss out singing 'UP and DOWN', put hands up and down
- Sing fourth time and miss out 'UP, DOWN, HALF WAY', put hands up, down and half way, in middle of body
- Last time sing really fast, missing out all above!

Positive thought for the week

Think about somebody you
would like to help.

You have been granted
three wishes.

Write down or draw an idea of how you can
really help somebody.

Share them with all of us on our
Circle Time Notice Board.

Laughing

Lesson objective: To explore happiness and sadness.
                     To be able to deal with sad situations.

Citizenship   To recognise, identify and deal with feelings in a positive way.

Introduction: Sing song (this either to be done before the Circle Time lesson in Literacy lesson
                    or at the beginning of Circle Time session).

Laughing bear (with music)

Laugh out loud, go on,
Laugh till you drop,
Giggle to yourself till,
Your tummy wants to pop!
POP! POP! GIGGLE! POP!
POP! POP! GIGGLE! POP!

Preparation for the lesson/Resources   Audio track – Laughing bear

Resources: Bear.

                          Problem box.

                          Bubbles.

Positive Thought Script: ✓

INTRODUCTION Group laugh Mime 	Laugh quietly and slowly in a circle, bring to a crescendo, making a loud raucous laugh, and then finish on the sound of a tambourine. Repeat. Mime a laugh individually, pass it on.
MAIN FEATURE 	"The thing that makes me laugh the most is…" "The funniest thing that ever happened to me was…"
ADDITIONAL IDEAS 	Teacher to put some known problems in bubble burst box, which are making children feel sad. Discuss any bubble burst problems from the box. Send bubbles round the circle. Use the bear to help with any problems. "Would it help if…"
LESSON ENDING ♪ Begin with part	Sing Laughing bear all the way through Then try and split into two parts. One part continues POP! POP! GIGGLE! POP! On POP! tap tummy with hand. The other part sings verse POP! POP! GIGGLE! POP! Then introduce verse

Positive thought for the week

Think of the last time you really laughed out loud
at something.

Shut your eyes and imagine how good it
made you feel. Laughter releases lots of energy in
our body which makes us feel better.

Try and enjoy this week and
see how many times you can laugh.

Enjoy your week!

Giggle to yourself till your
tummy wants to pop!

Pop! Pop! Giggle! Pop!
Pop! Pop! Giggle! Pop!

Mending

Lesson objective: To be able to learn how to retain friendships and how to be caring about one another.

Citizenship: To develop good relationships.

Introduction: Read poem and perform poem to rhythm (this either to be done before the Circle Time lesson in Literacy lesson or at the beginning of Circle Time session).

Mending bear

Mending, mending, mending bear,
Mend, Oh mend, my trouser tear!

Preparation for the lesson/Resources   Audio track – Mending bear

Preparation:	Find any alphabet song, i.e. ABC, DEFG, etc. (Pinocchio musical has a version and there are many choices).
	Calming music (any choice)
	Any music you can mime to.
Resources:	Bear.
	Bubbles.
Positive Thought Script:	✓

INTRODUCTION Mime (To music) 	Teacher to read the following script whilst music is playing (teachers may wish to expand script): "Pretend you are sewing a pair of ears on a teddy bear. Keep picking the bear up and checking him to see he looks alright. Waddle/move his ears about to make sure they are sewn on properly. Admire your finished bear, show it to the person next to you."
MAIN FEATURE Mending friendships 	How can we help people to stay friends and not to fall out? As a group or pairs, can we find some handy hints on friendships? e.g. Always listen to each other. Tell the truth. When the children have been given time to share their ideas, bring these ideas to the full circle. The teacher to list all the individual ideas. The children and teacher together decide which priority order to put them in. These can then be typed up and made into a poster for the wall. Send the bubbles around the circle. Finish the sentence: "I worry about friendships when…" Discuss if our set of handy hints can help with our worries.

ADDITIONAL IDEAS
 	
	'M' is the middle of the alphabet and it mends the two pieces of the alphabet together.
	
	Let us sing the alphabet song…A, B, C…etc. (any version!)
	
	Now we are going to play a game.
	(The teacher will hum the alphabet and stop at various places).
	The children try and guess where they have stopped.
	Let some children have a go at being 'the teacher'.
	
	Say the poem:
	
	    Mending, Mending, Mending bear,
	    Mend, Oh! Mend my trouser tear.

Each child will choose one word until the end of the poem is reached.

i.e. Child One – Mending   Child Two – Mending
      Child Three – Mending Child Four – Bear, etc.

Now the second time we do the same, but the child who should say 'trouser', changes it to something else with a tear.

e.g. jumper, skirt, jacket, sock, etc.

LESSON ENDING	Give the child next to you a back rub and receive one back and say "Friends are for caring."
	All sit down in a circle and hold hands and close your eyes.
	Listen to a calming piece of music.

Positive thought for the week

We all need friends
to care for us.

Draw or write about your favourite friend.

What makes them so special?

How many positive things can you draw or write?

Place it on our Circle Time Notice Board.

Noughts and Crosses

Lesson objective: To be able to understand fair play and treatment of others.

Citizenship: To recognise choices they can make and recognise the difference between right and wrong.

Introduction: Read poem and perform poem to rhythm (this either to be done before the Circle Time lesson in Literacy lesson or at the beginning of Circle Time session).

Noughts and Crosses bear

Your turn next, nought or cross?
Please put the right one, I don't mean to boss.
You've won too many games, it must be my turn,
My head is in a whirl and my stomach's in a churn.
Put a cross, put a cross, go on over there,
Then I'll put another one, I'll be a lucky bear.
If you listen to my thoughts, I'll win this next game,
Oh no! You've put a nought, Oh dear, what a shame!

Preparation for the lesson/Resources

Audio track – Noughts and Crosses bear

Preparation:	Prepare stickers, divide class into two halves. Put a 'O' (nought) sticker on one half of class. Put a 'X' (cross) sticker on the other half.
Resources:	Paper, pencils (for one between two).
	Bear.
	Problem box.
Positive Thought Script:	✓

INTRODUCTION

Game Discussion

"My favourite game is…"

"I don't like playing…because…"

Two minutes to play Noughts and Crosses with the partner next to you.

MAIN FEATURE
Fair Play Game

Go round the circle, children to label themselves alternatively Nought or Cross. (Or put labels on children).
Teacher – All the noughts cross the circle walking on their hands and knees and change places with another nought.

All the crosses, sit back and have a rest and have a sticker.
All the noughts jump on the spot (x ten).
All the crosses have a lie down.
All the noughts run round the outside of the circle and back to your place.
All the crosses pat yourselves on the back because you have been really good.

At this point, stop the game and ask the noughts how they are feeling?
They should make statements like:

"It's not fair." "We are doing all the work and the crosses are getting rewarded."

Use the opportunity to discuss fairness of games, the importance of making fair rules and not rules where one group of children feels disadvantaged. If appropriate, bring in sexism, boy or girl, and racist issue, black or white.

To end the game and discussion you need to ask the children how we can make the game fair.

The noughts no doubt will feel they deserve stickers, and the crosses can do a bit of the work! The noughts need to go away with the similar rewards to the crosses to make the game fair.

It needs to be discussed that one set of children were treated very unfairly in this game. Games should not be set up in this way, so that one set of children clearly will be discriminated against. A discussion with Infants on rules of games and how to make them fair would be an appropriate way to move forward. Children need to understand the rules are 'equal' to all, even if the game then has winners and losers. A discussion of treating each other fairly should be emphasised.

ADDITIONAL IDEAS

Teacher to bring problem box to the lesson, the following scenarios to be discussed:

Scenario 1
At playtime my two other best friends have started to play a game which they say can only be played as a pair. It is a ball game, which I would also like to play.

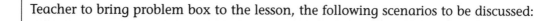

91

How can I get them to understand I would like to play, as I don't think this is fair?

Scenario 2
At dinnertime a group of boys play football on the special space we have for the game. However, they often carry the game on to where the girls are playing quieter games of elastic, skipping or other ball games, including football. It isn't fair! What can we do about it?

Children to come up with solutions to the above problems. A bear may be helpful to talk through. "Would it help if..."

LESSON ENDING

Say to the children, "Breathe in slowly and out slowly. Remember to keep your eyes closed and just listen to your breathing. Now wriggle your fingers, then relax them and let them be still. Now move your head slowly from side to side and now relax it and be still. Well done! Now we are ready to listen to our story."

Imagine going to a fairground, where everything around you is bright and colourful. You see the roundabouts, the Ferris Wheels, the game stalls where there are many prizes to be won.

You go over to one of the games, ten pence for five beanbags to knock over the cans. You think to yourself, "I can do it, Course I can do I, I'll have a go!" You take the beanbags excitedly and you tell yourself you **will** be able to knock over the cans.

You have your first shot, two cans fall, eight to go, a good start.

You have your second shot, Whoops! You miss, never mind, you still have three shots left.

You have your third shot, another two cans go, only six left to knock over.

Your fourth shot, another two down. Now the task is hard.

One shot left for four cans. Can you do it?

You stand still and breathe deeply. You calm yourself down, course you can do it. It's only a bit of fun, but it is possible!

You take your position ready to throw the beanbag.

You decide you'll throw after the count of three.

- deep breath
- steady yourself
- and throw.

You can hardly bear to look and suddenly, before you realise what is happening, an enormous teddy bear is being thrust into your arms. You've done it! You're a winner.

CONGRATULATIONS!

Feel really happy with your feeling of success.

At the end of the dream journey, remind the children to breathe slowly and listen to their own quiet breathing. Tell them, "Breathe in and out slowly and feel relaxed. Now wriggle your fingers then relax them and let them be still. Now move your head slowly from side to side and now relax it and be still. When you are ready, open your eyes. Well done everyone. You listened really well."

Allow for quiet reflection before moving on to the next stage.

Questions

- Have you ever won anything, either at a fair or in a competition?
- How did you feel?
- How do you feel when you lose?
- What important things do we need to think about when we lose game or in a competition?

Positive thought for the week

Think about the last time you felt 'on top of the world', either by winning a game, someone doing something nice for you or by achieving something well at home or school.

Think how this makes you feel – and how good you feel inside.

Hold on to this feeling of doing something good.

Write down or draw for us a time you felt 'on top of the world'.

Our notice board theme will be:

I felt 'on top of the world' when…

MUMS AND DADS

When were you most pleased or proud of your son or daughter?

Let us know so we can share it with all the class.

Orange drinking

Lesson objective: To explore the realms of space with our bodies and to join together with others in actions to create imaginative mime.

Citizenship: To play and work co-operatively.

Introduction: Read poem and perform poem to rhythm (this either to be done before the Circle Time lesson in Literacy lesson or at the beginning of Circle Time session).

Orange drinking bear

Drinking orange through a straw,
Is simply a wonderful thing,
Simply sitting in the sun
And a humming, ting-a-ling,
Ting-a-slurp-a-ling-a-slurp
A-slurp-a-ling-a-loo
Simply slurping through a straw
Is the best thing you can do!

Preparation for the lesson/Resources — Audio track – Orange drinking bear

Preparation: A drink of water or diluted orange for each child in class. (Be careful of additives – choose drink carefully).

Resources: Bear.

Bubbles.

Edible orange colouring (to make orange bubbles).

Tambourine.

Circle Time Notice Board Poster: ✓

INTRODUCTION	"My favourite drink is…" Children given a drink of water or orange and a straw and asked to see what happens when they blow in the straw either quickly or slowly.
MAIN FEATURE	Pretend you are in an orange bubble… from your orange drink. Push on the sides of your orange bubble to see if you can move the outer skin walls. Crouch down low in your orange bubble and become as small as you can. Blow on your orange bubble and make the sides change shape. Move around in your orange bubble, see what you can do in your orange bubble. Can you: • Stand on one leg • Turn round in circles • Dance • Stretch high or curl into a ball? Join with another orange bubble. Copy each other's actions like a mirror. After three, let us pop all our orange bubbles One, Two, Three, POP!!
ADDITIONAL IDEAS	Send orange bubbles (put in orange colouring) around the circle and ask the children to name one thing they are really pleased with themselves about, at the moment. Second time round, discuss or say anything they are disappointed with at present.

LESSON ENDING	Group yell – ORANGE BUBBLES!
	Build it up like a cauldron.
	ORANGE BUBBLE, ORANGE BUBBLE, ORANGE BUBBLE, ORANGE BUBBLE!
	Use arms to create orange bubble movements and make a class collage of bodies at the end on the final tambourine bang and to a final shout of ORANGE BUBBLE!
	To end the lesson, give the children the chance to have a fruit drink as a reward for their Circle Time.

Circle Time Notice Board

Bring in pictures or draw a picture of your favourite drinks this week.

Write some words to describe your favourite drink.

See if you can use alliteration, e.g.
Lovely, luscious, lilt.
Mouth-watering milk.
Captivating coca-cola

Mums and Dads... can you help
them with alliteration...
go on... have a go!

Party

Lesson objective: To understand that we are all different and need support. To understand that some situations cause stress on individuals.
To help us all enjoy leisure situations.

Citizenship: To identify and respect the difference between people.

Introduction: Read poem and perform poem to rhythm (this either to be done before the Circle Time lesson in Literacy lesson or at the beginning of Circle Time session).

Party bear

It's party time, hip hip hooray,
It's party time, a real fun day,
We've lots to eat, we'll share our food,
We'll say please and thank you, we won't be rude,
We'll laugh a lot, we'll dance and play,
It's party time, hip hip hooray!

Preparation for the lesson/Resources   Audio track – Party bear

Preparation: Prepare a 'Pass the Parcel' and put in forfeits, e.g. Say a poem, jump up and down ten times, dance, skip, etc.

Any music for 'Pass the Parcel'.

'Come to the Party' song, Game songs (or any party song).

Resources: Bear.

Skipping ropes.

Paper and pens.

Circle Time Notice Board Poster: ✓

INTRODUCTION 	Children may need help to read the forfeit. Wrap up a parcel and put forfeits in. The forfeits could include some party games, e.g. Say a poem, Jump up and down ten times, Dance, skip with a rope, etc. Pass the parcel around to music and stop the music for the paper to be unwrapped and forfeit to be undertaken.
MAIN FEATURE 	Sometimes people feel lonely at parties because they feel left out or shy. What sorts of things can we do to help each other to feel wanted and involved at parties? e.g. Partner some children together for some games (don't let the children choose partners). Ask the children before they come to the party, the sorts of games they like playing. Have quieter and lively games.
Activity A)	Let us make a list of the different types of games. e.g. Quieter Lively Wordsearch or Quiz Tig
Activity B)	In pairs, discuss all the food you would like to buy to put on the party table. Share ideas with the circle. Make a list to give to Mums and Dads to help with planning parties.
ADDITIONAL IDEAS 	"I love parties because…" "The thing I don't like about parties is…"
LESSON ENDING As a Group 	Make a list. Discuss most favourite and least favourite party food. Sing, 'Come to a Party', Game Songs (or any party song).

Circle Time Notice Board

Parties are fun – most of the time.

Have you got a photograph from a party you have been to or have had?

Place it on our Circle Time notice board.

Would you like to draw a party
picture to remind you of something
you did?

Whose birthday is it this
week or next?

NAMES: _____

_____

_____

_____

_____

Quiet reading

Lesson objective: To understand that we all need personal quiet space and to discuss ways of creating this.

Citizenship: To recognise how their behaviour affects other people.

Introduction: Read poem and perform poem to rhythm (this either to be done before the Circle Time lesson in Literacy lesson or at the beginning of Circle Time session).

Quiet reading bear

Sh! Sh! for quiet bear,
He's reading quietly, Sh!
Sh! He's snuggled up with a friend, Sh! Sh! Sh!

Sh! Sh! for reading bear,
He's having a quiet time, Sh!
Sh! He needs us to leave him alone, Sh! Sh! Sh!

Sh! Sh! we all need quiet,
We need quiet right now, Sh!
Sh! We need to have a time on our own, Sh! Sh! Sh!

Sh! Sh! Please go away,
I need to be quiet, Sh!
Sh! I'll see you later, Ok? Sh! Sh! Sh!

Preparation for the lesson/Resources   Audio track – Quiet reading bear

Preparation: Need to prepare paints, paper, or drawing crayons and paper, or magazines and glue to make a group picture.
Any quiet music.

Resources: Bear.

Scissors.

Pens and paper.

Tambourine.

Positive Thought Script: ✓

INTRODUCTION 	"My favourite quiet place is…" "If I had a secret place it would be…" "Things that make me feel peaceful are…"
MAIN FEATURE 	**In groups** Make a group picture of a quiet place. (Draw, Paint, Model). Decide what needs to be in it. ⎫ Make a list of all the items needed. ⎬ You may wish to do this at the end of the lesson in a separate art lesson Plan it carefully. Think of colours carefully. ⎪ Discuss the finished quiet place pictures. ⎭ What is it that stops us having quiet moments to ourselves? Let us make a collective list of all the things that make us unable to concentrate, sit quietly or work quietly. Now let's look at some of these problems and use our bear to help us solve some of these problems. e.g. Someone talking to us in lessons – problem. Ask them to stop – solution. Ignore them or ask to move places – solution.
ADDITIONAL IDEAS	**FOLLOW-UP IDEAS USING HALL SPACE** Circle escape (best performed in hall). A child to go into the centre of the circle and try to escape. The rules are: As the child runs towards the outside of the circle, the other children put their arms across the gap to make a barrier. The child is not to push through the barrier.

The child must try and trick the children, dodging through a gap if possible.

After a few tries, the child receives a back rub or pat and then another child tries to escape.

Freedom Run

Everyone into the hall, find a space. Run round, avoiding bumping into anyone, arms outstretched shouting FREEDOM.

On the bang of a tambourine FREEZE. Now get into groups of four to six and form a tightly packed group where no-one can escape.

Shout TRAPPED.

Bang of tambourine, run round again, arms outstretched, shouting FREEDOM.

On bang of tambourine, regroup four to six, shout TRAPPED, etc

LESSON ENDING	Form a circle and lie down to a quiet piece of music.
	Very slowly start actions, slowly moving round the circle (as Mexican wave).
	Sit up one by one...Lie down one by one. Legs up and in...Legs down and out...Turn over...Turn back...Arms over head...Arms back...Repeat actions.

Positive thought for the week

Imagine you had a secret place that you could go to, to be really quiet.

Imagine in that secret place you had hidden lots of your favourite books.

This place makes you feel really relaxed and happy.

No-one can disturb you in this secret place and you can read in peace.

Which favourite books or comics would you take to your favourite place?

How does this quiet place make you feel?

Enjoy the feeling of relaxation.

Our notice board says:

Favourite books for a secret place:

....

....

....

....

....

Relaxing

Lesson objective: To enable us to discover how to enjoy quality relaxation times.

Citizenship: To take part in discussion with one person.

Introduction: Read poem and perform poem to rhythm (this either to be done before the Circle Time lesson in Literacy lesson or at the beginning of Circle Time session).

Relaxing bear

Relax, go on, sit back in the chair,
Put your feet up, like Brandon, you don't need to stare,
Find a position, to let your body feel free,
Is it crossing your legs, arms draped on the settee?

Relax, go on, let your cares float away,
If you learn to relax, you'll enjoy all your day,
Lie on the floor, let your body feel light,
If your friends arrive, just shut your eyes tight.

They'll think you're asleep, they'll creep out of sight,
And then you'll relax, you'll just get it right!

Preparation for the lesson/Resources   Audio track – Relaxing bear

Preparation: Any quiet music you feel is relaxing and creative to paint to.

Resources: Bear.

                                Paper (for painting) and a choice of paints, brushes, etc.

                                Problem box.

Positive Thought Script: ✓

INTRODUCTION To be completed in an Art lesson	Close your eyes and lie down. Listen to a quiet piece of music. Think how it makes you feel. What can you see as the music is playing? Put a piece of paper in front of every child and a choice of colours. When the music has finished, discuss how the music made them feel… What did they think about as they listened to it. Put the music on again and ask the children to paint ideas that come into their heads. Tell the children to think carefully of the way they do the strokes on the paper, to ensure they capture the mood of the music. When all pictures are dry, discuss at Circle Time.
MAIN FEATURE 	Bring pictures to Circle Time that had been prepared in Art lesson. Ask the children to describe their pictures and discuss the colours they have chosen. Ask them if they are pleased with the end results, or if anything would improve the quality of their Pictures. Put the pictures down on the floor, play the music again and ask the children to look at each other's pictures by moving around and listen to the music to see if they fit in with the music. Back to Circle Time games, prepare for musical Dream journey. Now listen to another quiet piece of music with your eyes shut. As the music plays, paint a story in your mind. Think of the colours you use carefully. At the end of the music you will be asked to describe your story and the colours you used. At end of music children share ideas.
ADDITIONAL IDEAS 	Tell a friend what you like to do to relax. Do you like going for a walk? Do you like playing on your computer, reading, riding your bicycle, watching T.V. etc? Do you relax with your family, have a meal together, play a game? Share ideas with the whole group. Talk about quality relaxation. From the previous week, share with the group some bubble burst problems, which stopped us relaxing, because we don't have enough quiet space. Use the bear to help solve the problems.

LESSON ENDING

Game, like Simon Says.

Tell the children. If teacher says 'DO THIS', you must copy.

If teacher says 'DO THAT', you must not copy.

See how many children can copy at the right time.

Pass leader on to a child.

Positive thought for the week

(Music to our ears)

Which music helps you relax or makes you feel happy?

Is it the sound of the birds singing in the morning?

Is it the sound of a train as it moves swiftly passed?

Is it the sound of a church bell?

Or is it music you have at home?

Write down your favourite sound or music.
Tell us how it makes you feel.

Stripy

Lesson objective: To understand that colours create moods and feelings and enhance telling stories.

Citizenship: To listen to other people and play and work co-operatively.

Introduction: Sing the song (this either to be done before the Circle Time lesson in Literacy lesson or at the beginning of Circle Time session).

Stripy bear (with music)

My friend stripy bear, your stripes are like rings,
That you throw at a fair and win goldfish and things.
Your legs, are so long, you could win a fast race,
You could run a long marathon and keep up the pace.

Let's learn all your colours, let's give it a try,
We'll take a deep breath and we'll try not to sigh...

From the top...from the top,
Let's try not to drop.
Orange, white, orange, yellow, orange, red, orange, grey.
orange, pink, orange, green, orange, yellow, orange, pink.
orange, grey, orange, pink, orange, green, orange, peach.
orange, white, orange, yellow, orange, pink, orange, grey, orange.

Can you do it? Can you do it? I bet you do it fast,
Take a breath at the start and see if you can last!
(repeat orange, white, etc.)

Preparation for the lesson/Resources

Preparation:

Resources:

Positive Thought Script:

Audio track – Stripy bear

Prepare Stripy bear's stripes.

Cut out 33 stripes and have a list of order – Stripy bear's colours on A4/ A3 sheet on CD.

Prepare large Stripy bear picture with colours in order or a long stripy scarf in colour order.

Bear.

✓

INTRODUCTION

1. orange 18. grey
2. white 19. orange
3. orange 20. pink
4. yellow 21. orange
5. orange 22. green
6. red 23. orange
7. orange 24. peach
8. grey 25. orange
9. orange 26. white
10. pink 27. orange
11. orange 28. yellow
12. green 29. orange
13. orange 30. pink
14. yellow 31. orange
15. orange 32. grey
16. pink 33. orange
17. orange

Give out Stripy bear's stripes around circle (33 Colours). (In order of colours)

Some children to receive possibly two colours.

Have a list of colours in order.

Need large picture of Stripy bear, colours painted in order (or a long stripy scarf, colours in order).

As the teacher passes her finger down the colours without speaking, one by one the children wait their turns and put the colours in order on the floor. The children should be sat in order, so this should not be too complicated.

Once this is completed, all clap at such an accomplishment.

Now try and repeat the procedure without the children sitting in order.

Try and do it without the teacher putting her finger down the colours, the children reading the colours for themselves. (Teacher to keep an eye in case they get lost!).

Collect together:

17 orange stripes

2 white stripes

3 yellow stripes

1 red stripe

3 grey stripes

4 pink stripes

2 green stripes

1 peach stripe

Every child keeps *one* of Stripy bear's colours for next game.

Play change places game.

e.g. All oranges bounce like a ball across the circle and change places.

All reds dance like flames across the circle.

All yellows and peaches roll like a lemon and peach across the circle.

All greens move like long spiky grass across the circle.

All whites bark like a white dog across the circle.

All greys spin like a meteorite across the circle.

All pinks strut like a flamingo with long legs across the circle.

MAIN FEATURE

Begin a colour story around the circle. The children have to add something to the story and there must be a colour in their sentence.

e.g.

One morning, the *golden* sunshine came peeping through my curtains.

I opened my *blue* curtains and said, "good morning *golden* sunshine."

I got dressed quickly and wore my *pink* trousers and *white* T-shirt.

I came downstairs to eat my breakfast, *orange* juice and a *yellow* banana.

Another version of this would be to give the child a colour and an object to put into the story.

LESSON ENDING

Colour and moods.

Shout or say the sentence and use your bodies to express the words. Make the end of the sentence a 'freeze frame' of your mood.

- Red makes you angry

- Blue makes you sad
- Green makes you peaceful
- Orange is fun
- Purple is a monster
- Brown is dreamy
- Black is scary.

Try as a group and then individually, or in a small group.

Positive thought for the week

Our journey to school can be fun!

Make your journey as much fun as you can.

Can you try and look carefully at the things you
see on the way to school in the morning.

How do these things make you feel?

Which is your favourite thing –
no matter how small?

Draw your route.
Use colours to help.

Place it on our Circle Time Notice Board.

Tall

Lesson objective: To enable us to feel confident in our own capabilities.

Citizenship: To recognise how their behaviour affects other people.

Introduction: Read poem and perform poem to rhythm (this either to be done before the Circle Time lesson in Literacy lesson or at the beginning of Circle Time session).

Tall bear

I'm tall, I really am,
Stand me on a wall and you'll see,
I can stretch, I really can,
Stand me on a chair, let me be!

You're small, you really are,
Now you know just what it's like,
I'm getting down, cos I'm tall inside,
Let's have a ride on my bike!

Preparation for the lesson/Resources

Audio track – Tall bear

Resources: Bear.

Digital camera.

Tambourine.

Positive Thought Script: ✓

INTRODUCTION

Orally pass round large and small words, alternatively.

e.g. Large elephant, small mouse, large house, small nest, large tree, small flower, large pole, small …

Children use their bodies to show large or small.

i.e. Stand – tall.

Crouch – small.

MAIN FEATURE

Sometimes things make us feel 'small' and not very important. To make ourselves feel 'tall' and confident again, we need to find solutions to our 'small' problems.

We need to think about our actions towards each other. Sometimes people feel 'small' or not confident when they are with us because we are not kind and thoughtful.

Let us brainstorm some of our problems that worry us and see if we can come up with solutions to help *our confidence grow*.

Make a list of small problems, e.g. worried about spellings, not enjoying school dinner.

Now use our bear to try to help solve some of them.

Children and teacher to look at problems and choose some to solve.

Use language, "Would it help if…"

"The thing I do best of all is…"

ADDITIONAL IDEAS

Put children in groups of four or five.

Tell the children they are making objects in a group.

Give instructions, in ten seconds make…

Large {
a Loch Ness monster.
a Castle.
a winding path.
a dragon's mouth.

Teacher counts – 10, 9, 8, 7, 6, 5, 4, 3, 2, 1

Bangs tambourine and

says 'freeze!'

Small {
peas in a pod.
candles flickering.
a curled up hedgehog.

10, 9, 8, 7…

Children often like you to come round with a pretend camera, to take a picture of their finished collage. On occasions, have digital camera to show them final results.

LESSON ENDING ☺	All hold hands and close your eyes.
	Think of all the things you are really good at.
	Through our circle of friendship, let us pass our happy thoughts on to each other and feel confident, happy and strong.
	Send a friendly squeeze round the circle.

Positive thought for the week

Think happy thoughts!

What makes you happy?

Tell us about your happy thought for the week.

Write about it and put it on our special Circle Time Notice Board.

Mums and Dads, do you want to help us?
What makes you really happy?

Umbrella

Lesson objective: To use a variety of games to explore working together as groups. To use Dream journeys to create a feeling of calmness, fun and contentment.

Citizenship: To share their opinions on things that matter to them and explain their views.

Introduction: Read poem and perform poem to rhythm (this either to be done before the Circle Time lesson on Literacy or at the beginning of Circle Time session).

Umbrella Bear

Umbrella sun,
Umbrella rain,
Umbrella showers,
On window pane.

Umbrella colours,
Umbrella twirl,
Umbrella rainbow,
Over smiling girl.

Umbrella fun,
Umbrella muddles,
Umbrella dancing,
In muddy puddles.

Umbrella happy,
Umbrella sad,
Umbrella sharing,
With mum or dad.

Umbrella running,
Umbrella race,
Umbrella dog,
In Umbrella chase.

Umbrella love,
Umbrella care,
Umbrella down,
If you dare!

Preparation for the lesson/Resources — Audio track – Umbrella bear

Preparation:
For each individual child, prepare an umbrella colour card.

Ensure there are four colours evenly distributed across the class – red, yellow, green or blue.

Prepare for eight children a letter card to spell the word

Umbrella – [U] [M] [B] [R] [E] [L] [L] [A]

Resources:
Bear.

Large paper and felt-tip pens.

Some hand drums and tambourines. Teacher tambourine.

Positive Thought Script: ✓

INTRODUCTION

"If I had a magic umbrella I would…"

Words that remind me of rain, e.g. puddle, splash, wet, damp, ducks, drip, etc.

MAIN FEATURE

Say to the children, "Breathe in slowly and out slowly. Remember to keep your eyes closed and just listen to your breathing. Now wriggle your fingers, then relax them and let them be still. Now move your head slowly from side to side and now relax it and be still. Well done! Now we are ready to listen to our story."

Now imagine you are walking down a leafy lane with your friend, the sun is shining in the deep blue sky and the birds are singing in the trees above you. At the end of the lane is a beautiful field full of golden, yellow buttercups. You love to play in this field with your friend, as there is a gentle hill which you love to run towards and then roly-poly all the way to the bottom of the hill. How you always giggle as you reach the bottom and then run to the top to try it again.

As the field comes into sight, you start to run….you both have a race to see who will reach the buttercups first. As you enter the field you feel happy and carefree and you run until you reach the hill and then fall into your roly-polys, over and over you go, laughing, wondering who will get to the bottom first. Down and down you roll, you see golden buttercups flashing past you, you are having so much fun you don't notice the first splash of rain, nor the second, but suddenly a downpour of rain makes you both jump up and dash for shelter under the trees. You shelter there hoping the rain will soon stop and you huddle together. Your golden field of buttercups looks as if it is crying, golden tears rest on their petals, and then gently trickle to the ground.

They look beautiful and you are fascinated at how the rain makes them sparkle and they almost look magical.

Then, without warning, the sun comes out, the rain stops, and the petals sparkle in the golden sunshine.

Time to go, hand in hand, two friends together you make your way up the golden carpet, to return another day, in the sunshine. You have had a really fun day, even if it did rain!

At the end of the dream journey, remind the children to breathe slowly and listen to their own quiet breathing. Tell them, "Breathe in and out slowly and feel relaxed. Now wriggle your fingers then relax them and let them be still. Now move your head slowly from side to side and now relax it and be still. When you are ready, open your eyes. Well done everyone. You listened really well."

Allow for quiet reflection before moving on to the next stage.

Questions

- What could you see, hear, touch, taste and smell in the beautiful field of buttercups?
- How does it feel to run a race down a hill?
- Do you feel excited?
- What are your thoughts as you race a friend?
- Describe the field of buttercups as the rain fell on their petals. How did the buttercups look?

ADDITIONAL IDEAS	Give out some cards with different coloured umbrellas on (red, yellow, green and blue).
	Also give eight children an individual letter to spell U M B R E L L A
	Tell the children to look at their cards but not to show them to anyone else.
	Begin game – All the red umbrellas stand up, twirl your imaginary umbrellas across the circle and change places with another red umbrella.
	Stand up – All the blue umbrellas hop across the circle, out of the rain , and change places with another blue umbrella.
	Stand up – All the yellow umbrellas, stretch your umbrella high and twirl round on the spot.
	Stand up – Green umbrellas, pretend you are shaking your umbrella, which is full of raindrops, give it a really good shake, opening it and closing it. Now change places with another green umbrella.
Instruction	All letter cards stand up – Letter cards, run to the centre of the circle, hold up your letter, in 10 seconds letter spell the word 'umbrella' correctly
	Teacher counts down – 10, 9, 8, 7, etc.
	At end of game, if there is time, change the cards so children receive a different one and let a child call the instructions.
LESSON ENDING	Beginning low on the ground and getting taller and taller and end with arms outstretched like an umbrella.
	Say low, "Um...Um...Um" Louder and grow, "Um...Um" "UMBRELLA!"
	Now try THUNDERSTORM.
	(use drums or banging on legs for effect).
	How about lightning! ✗

Positive thought for the week

Imagine all week the beautiful buttercup field in the dream journey with golden yellow buttercups.

How did it make you feel?

Can you capture it in a drawing?

Place it on our Circle Time Notice Board.

Very happy

Lesson objective: To understand how to deal with emotions of happiness and sadness (followed up from Laughing).

Citizenship: That they belong to various groups and communities, such as family and school.

Introduction: Read poem and perform poem to rhythm (this either to be done before the Circle Time lesson in Literacy lesson or at the beginning of Circle Time session).

Very happy bear

Very happy bear
Happy bear
Bear
Bear very happy.
Bear happy
Bear
Very bear happy
Very bear
Bear.
Very very very
Happy happy happy
Bear bear bear
Very happy bear
Very!

Preparation: Box of instruments.

Story – Dabbit Day (on CD).

Resources: Bear.

A red hat and a yellow hat.

Positive Thought Script: ✓

INTRODUCTION

Each child chooses a word, **very**, **happy** or **bear**, it does not matter which word they choose, it is not to be recited in a set order.

Now beginning round the circle, each child says their word to make a new poem of Very happy bear.

e.g. Child One: **very**; Child Two: **very**; Child Three: **happy**;

      Child Four: **bear**; Child Five: **bear**; Child Six: **very**;

      Child Seven: **very**, etc.

Repeat and ask them to choose a different word, make it a fun poem.

Use instruments to make it more fun.

MAIN FEATURE

 (Pairs)

Tell a friend about one of the happiest days you have ever spent.

Explain why you were so happy and all the events that took place.

Ask for volunteers. Include moments from your family life and friendships.

Circle discussion.

What makes us sad?

What can we do to help us become happy again when we are sad?

Use the bear to suggest,

   "Would it help if next time you are sad…"

Hat game, use two different coloured hats, e.g. red and yellow hats. A child has both hats in front of them. One hat is to represent sad things (e.g. red hat, the other hat is to represent solutions (e.g. yellow hat).

e.g. Hat One: "Sometimes I am sad when my mum shouts and

    (Red Hat)   becomes angry."

    Hat Two: "So I try to cheer her up by tidying my room and

    (Yellow Hat) then she smiles."

    Hat One: "I was really sad when my hamster died."

    (Red Hat)

    Hat Two: "My mum and I buried it in the garden and then I

    (Yellow Hat) went for a bike ride, which cheered me up."

Children can volunteer to begin with the demonstration.

Alternatively it can be played: Child One has problem (Red Hat)
                                     Child Two volunteers solution (Yellow Hat)

Yellow Hat to be placed in middle for volunteers for solutions.

Teacher may also wish to explain that sometimes it is o.k to be sad and that we need to be able to understand when these feelings are acceptable, e.g. bereavement.

LESSON ENDING Story	Read 'Dabbit Day'. Think about what has happened in this story between the friends, discuss friendships. Do you think 'Dabbit Day' is a good title?

Dabbit Day

"It's a roly poly rabbit day today!" shouted Dee Dee the rabbit
who lived at the top of Marland Hill.
"Roly poly rabbit days are my favourite days. They make me very happy.
They happen every Sunday when the sun is shining," he told a passing butterfly.

"Today is a perfect day."
"I wonder where Raggles is? He should be here by now."
He looked around for his friend.
"Hello Dee Dee," said Raggles the dog. "It's a roly poly
dog day today," he teased.

Dee Dee twitched his ears before he replied.
"Now Raggles, I've told you before. It's called roly poly
rabbit day. Rabbits love to roly poly."
Dee Dee paused for a moment.

"Dogs...well...dogs...they love to join in," he whispered
cautiously, not wanting to upset his friend.
"Anyway, rabbits have special days named after them ...
so there!" Dee Dee said finally.

"Oh who cares what it is called?" said Raggles.
"Let's roll! Last to the bottom is a drooping dandelion."
And off they went, rolling down Marland Hill.
"Wheeeee!" said Dee Dee – "this is great fun."
"Beejaggles!" shouted Raggles – "this is fantastic."
"A draw," they agreed at the bottom of the hill, because
no one really wanted to be a drooping dandelion.

Suddenly, Bazal bear arrived at the top of Marland Hill.
"Hello Raggles, hello Dee Dee," he shouted
as he waved his hand.
"It's roly poly dabbit day," he said chuckling to himself.

Raggles and Dee Dee hurried to the top of Marland Hill.
"What's a dabbit day?" said Raggles amused by
his friend's silly little ways.
"Everyone knows what a dabbit day is. It's a rabbit and
dog day mixed together," said Bazal bear.
"Okay," said Dee Dee, "You win, dabbit day it is. We'll
call it roly poly dabbit day."

"Let's roly poly dabbit," said Bazal.
"Let's go for it!" shouted Raggles and Dee Dee together.
"Last to the bottom is a drooping dandelion," Raggles
reminded his friends.
"Don't you mean a drooping dabbit dandelion," Bazal
said smiling.

"We'll roll after 3 dabbits," said Dee Dee.
"DABBIT, DABBIT, DABBIT!" they all shouted together.
Which made them all very happy and excited.
"Wheeeee!" said Dee Dee.
"Bejaggles!" shouted Raggles.
"Jinglejal!" Bazal said, to join in with the fun.

And of course it was a draw, because no-one wanted to
be a drooping dabbit dandelion and everyone went away very happy,
as it had been a very exciting day.

124

Positive thought for the week

When did you last play in the park?

When did you last play your favourite game?

How did it make you feel?

Draw us a picture for our Circle Time Notice Board
of your favourite day with friends.

Write a sentence:

I felt good because...

WOW

Lesson objective: To feel positive about self and others and to recognise each others strengths.

Citizenship: To listen to other people and play and work co-operatively.

Introduction: Read poem and perform poem to rhythm (this either to be done before the Circle Time lesson in Literacy lesson or at the beginning of Circle Time session).

WOW bear

WOW! says Blinkle,
Your singing was great,
WOW! says Blinkle,
You're sitting so straight,
WOW! says Blinkle,
Your behaviour is just right,
WOW! says Blinkle,
You look happy and bright,
WOW! says Blinkle,
You can reach for the stars,
WOW! says Blinkle,
You could land on Mars!

Preparation for the lesson/Resources   Audio track – WOW bear

Preparation: Teacher: Prepare a class list with something positive to say about each child.

                                Find a special or favourite song to sing.

Resources: Bear.

                                Ball (football size).

                                Piece of paper and pen for each child.

Positive Thought Script: ✓

INTRODUCTION

Mexican wave

"I use 'WOW' when…"

All lie down in the circle, hands above heads, sit up one by one and say "WOW." The second time round the circle lie down when it is your turn and say "WOW."

MAIN FEATURE

 Positive phrases

Roll a ball across the circle to a friend and say something positive to them. For example, "WOW Jack…you have got lovely eyes."

"WOW Paula, you are good at running."

"WOW Saima, I like your name."

Give each child a piece of paper with a child's name on it, from the class.

Ensure all children have their names written down and no-one is left out. Write or draw something positive about the person and then give them back their piece of paper.

Teacher to say something positive about every child in the circle, as the bear is passed around. (pre-prepare these so you do not hesitate).

At the end of the session all children should feel praised.

e.g. "Danielle, you deserve a WOW because your story writing has been really good this week."

"Jamie, you have been really well behaved this week, well done!"

The children are then given out stickers.

ADDITIONAL IDEAS

Tell each other about someone who is really special.

Explain all the reasons which make them special.

List all the things that make people special, e.g. kindness, caring, helpful.

LESSON ENDING

Choose a special or favourite song to sing.

Positive thought for the week

Say '**WOW**' this week at anything
that is special.

Add your 'WOWS' to our Circle Time
Notice Board.

WOW!

Xylophone

Lesson objective: To be able to recognise that others benefit from our help or need our kind thoughts.

Citizenship: To share their opinion on things that matter to them.

Introduction: Read poem and perform poem to rhythm (this either to be done before the Circle Time lesson in Literacy lesson or at the beginning of Circle Time session).

Xylophone bear

Play the xylophone, if you choose,
Feel the rhythm, sing the blues,
Up and down the keys you slide,
The notes dance out, you feel them inside,
Rhythm fast, rhythm slow,
Feel that beat, let the music flow.

Preparation for the lesson/Resources   Audio track – Xylophone bear

Preparation: 3 prizes: A – Sticker.

                                        B – Carrot.

                                        C – Crayons.

                           (or any prizes the teacher wishes, including a silly prize).

Resources: Bear.

                           Xylophone.

                           Bubbles.

                           Problem box.

Positive Thought Script: ✓

INTRODUCTION

One child is 'on' and goes out of the room.

One child who remains in the circle is chosen and told they are a magic lamp, with a genie inside.

Ten children stand like lamps (similar to 'I am a little teapot', hand on hip, other arm forms a spout).

The child then comes back in the room and chooses one child and rubs their arms saying, "Magic Genie speak to me, grant me please, wishes three."

The child has three tries at finding the correct lamp.

The incorrect lamps reply, "No genie at home."

If the child is correct the genie replies, "Genie at home, what is your wish master or mistress, wish A, B or C?" The child then has to choose.

The teacher has prepared three prizes, e.g.

    A – Sticker)   At the end of each game,

    B – Carrot)   the letters are changed round

    C – Crayons)

The child receives the prize they have chosen.

The correct teapot or lamp then goes out for their turn.

If the child does not get it right, they can choose anyone to go outside.

MAIN FEATURE

Xylophones are often magical in fairy stories. In front of us we have a magical xylophone. If we pass it round and play on it we could perhaps make a wish.

You can make a wish out loud, try and make a kind wish, e.g. I wish my gran wouldn't keep having pains in her legs. I wish my mum could have someone to help her clean the house. Or you can have a silent wish.

Play the xylophone first, make your wish and then, at the same time, we will pass our bubbles round, if you have a worry or a wish, blow the bubbles high and see if they can take the worry or wish away from you. Don't forget, if you really need help, you can write your worry in the bubble time box, or ask to speak to your teacher about something.

e.g.

> I am scared
> at nights. Can
> you help me?
>> Javid

LESSON ENDING	*Group Yell* Abracadabra (other suggested magic words) End on a group hug

Positive thought for the week

Tonight… before you go to bed… look for a star and make a wish.

Wish for something good to happen to someone who really needs it.

You might wish to make someone feel better, you might wish for someone to cheer up.

Look at that star and wish really hard… and let's hope your wish comes true.

Yawning

Lesson objective: To recognise that some of us are scared of the dark and need strategies to deal with this.

Citizenship: To deal with feelings in a positive way.

Introduction: Read poem and perform poem to rhythm (this either to be done before the Circle Time lesson in Literacy lesson or at the beginning of Circle Time session).

Yawning bear

If you open your mouth a yawn comes just see,
I know I'm not tired, but it takes over me,
I try not to yawn, I try so hard to look bright,
But a yawn creeps over me, no matter how I fight,
It starts in my throat and vibrates over my tongue,
It forces open my teeth and I know it's wrong.
But I open my mouth, like a great hippopotamus,
And I put my head back and I try not to fuss-a-muss
I stretch my arms out and then say most politely,
Excuse me my friends, which they accept quite rightly!

Preparation for the lesson/Resources   Audio track – Yawning bear

Resources: Bear, puppet.

                           Bubbles.

Positive Thought Script: ✓

INTRODUCTION	Pass on a yawn; smile; frown; stamp. "I feel tired when…" "I feel lively when…"
MAIN FEATURE	Tell your friend about the last time somebody came to stay at your house, or when you stayed at a friend's house. Did you stay up late? Did you watch a DVD? Play games? Have a midnight feast? Was it fun? Share some ideas with the whole circle. "Sometimes I can't get to sleep because…" "Would it help if…"
LESSON ENDING	There was once a little girl called Sally Sleep-a-Lot and her best friend was called Dolly Don't-Sleep-Much. Now Sally Sleep-a-Lot was always dozing, sometimes she even dozed in class and her teacher Mrs Sing-a-Lot, said to Sally, "Sally, what time did you get to bed last night?" "You're always tired and sleepy, it really isn't good enough." But Sally always replied the same, "Mrs Sing-a-Lot, I always go to bed early, but I have such wonderful dreams. Dreams of Fairyland and magical places. Fields of beautiful flowers, sparkling streams and of animals that talk. Any minute I can, I just want to close my eyes to get back into those lovely dreams." Now Dolly-Don't-Sleep-Much, was also always dozing in class, but this was because she didn't sleep and Mrs Sing-a-Lot knew that Dolly was really scared when she went to bed. "I'll tell you what" said Mrs Sing-a-Lot brightly, "I know a way you could both help each other. Sally, you don't need to be asleep to tell us of your lovely dreams. We can end each day with some of your special stories and then anyone who worries when they go to bed, can try and think each evening about your ideas in your dream world. I will help these dreams travel home with you by sprinkling you with my special magic dust. Then when you all start having super dreams, we can share some of them." The children thought this was a super idea, and soon they were all coming to school with super ideas from their dream world… and Sally Sleep-a-Lot became re-named Sally Share-Your-Dreams and Dolly Don't-Sleep-Much became Dolly Has-Sweet-Dreams. Mrs Sing-a-Lot, certainly did sing as she busied herself around the classroom, as the children were working hard. Her class was full of contented, happy children, and they knew they had a treat in store for them at the end of each day, as they went home with a pocketful of magical dreams.

Questions

- Which magical dreams have you had?
  Share some of your dreams with each other.
- What should we do if we can't get to sleep?
  Make a list of things to make us sleep.

Positive thought for the week

Try and think about what you want to dream about before you go to bed.

Make it a really happy dream and be relaxed.

Have a lovely dream this week.

Place your dream picture on our Circle Time Notice Board

Zig Zag

Lesson objective: To recognise that language does not need to be a barrier and that we communicate by feelings and expression.

Citizenship: To take part in discussions.

Introduction: Read poem and perform poem to rhythm (this either to be done before the Circle Time lesson in Literacy lesson or at the beginning of Circle Time session).

Zig Zag Bear...Zig Zag Zoo

Zig Zag...Zig Zag Zoo,
Twiddly, Diddly, Wiggly, Woo,
Zig Zog...Zig Zog Zug,
Wuggly, Buggly, Duggly, Dug.
Zig Zag...Zig Zag Zonk,
Doggly, Hoggly, Boggly, Gonk!
Zig Zag...Bear Zag Zoo,
I can see him, Zag, can you?

INTRODUCTION 	Children put into approximately groups of five or six. Tell the children to count backwards 10-0 (10, 9, 8, 7, 6, 5, 4, 3, 2, 1, 0) to make the following shape: • Make an interesting Zig- Zag shape, teacher counts 10, 9, 8, 7… • Make a Zebra Crossing, 10, 9, 8, 7… • Make the word Buzz, 10, 9, 8, 7… • Make a Zebra, 10, 9, 8, 7… • Make a different Zig- Zag, 10, 9, 8, 7… On the number '0' children asked to freeze. Teacher looks at each shape in turn. Say a nonsense word… Say your favourite word.
MAIN FEATURE 	Put the class in two groups. Read Zig Zag bear poem in two parts, as if it were a conversation. Each group takes one line at a time. Say the poem as if you are angry. Say the poem as if you are asking questions. Say the poem as if you are really excited. In pairs. Have a nonsense conversation with your friend. Use expressions, angry, happy, excited, puzzled, worried to make your conversation more interesting. *Situation One*: Try a situation, e.g. You have just lost your child in the supermarket and you are explaining to the manager what they look like and where you lost them. Don't forget to use all nonsense words. Use your arms for expression. *Situation Two*: Someone has just hit your car with their car. Discuss this angrily with them, using nonsense conversation.

ADDITIONAL IDEAS 	One child leaves the room. The other children are told that the word Zig Zag means hold their arms out in front and cross them. If the word is said again, they change over position of arms and cross them. One child in the group is told to do something in addition at the same time as crossing their arms, e.g. cross legs at same time, tap foot, wink, nod their head. The child then returns and gives the instruction Zig Zag. They keep saying it (five times at most) to try and find the odd one out. If they don't find the child, they own up and then it is that child's turn to go out. If they do find the child, they may choose who they wish to go out.
LESSON ENDING 	All those wearing blue, Zig Zag across the circle into another place. All those wearing red, walk across the circle, shake hands with someone and say, wuggly buggly. All those wearing... (other ideas) Change places and smile at another and say wuggly buggly. All those wearing... Change places and back rub another and say wuggly buggly.

Circle Time Notice Board

Are you looking forward to your holiday?

Draw or write about your favourite
holiday memories.

Bring in brochures of your holiday for this year.

Tell us about what you are going to do in
the holidays.

Appendix: Stripy Bear's Knitting Pattern

by Irene Weatherhead

Double Knitting Wool – No.9 needles

Head

Use cream wool

Begin at end of nose and cast on 6sts. loosely

1st row, Inc k wise into every st = 12 sts.

P1 row

Next row, K1, inc in next 10 sts, k1 = 22 sts.

P1 row

Shape Nose

1st row, K1, m1, k7, m1, k6, m1, k7, m1, k1 = 26 sts.

2nd row and every following alternate row – Purl

3rd row, K1, m1, k9, m1, k6, m1, k9, m1, k1 = 30 sts.

5th row, K1, m1, k11, m1, k6, m1, k11, m1, k1 = 34 sts.

7th row, K1, m1, k13, m1, k6, m1, k13, m1, k1 = 38 sts.

9th row, K1, m1, k15, m1, k6, m1, k15, m1, k1 = 42 sts.

Next row, 10th row, (p1 p2tog) 6 times, p6 (p2tog, p1) 6 times = 30 sts.

Shape Head – change to brown wool

1st row, K11, m1, k1, m1, k6, m1, k1, m1, k11 = 34 sts.

2nd and every following alternate row – Purl

3rd row, K12, m1, k1, m1, k8, m1, k1, m1, k12 = 38 sts.

5th row, K13, m1, k1, m1, k10, m1, k1, m1, k13 = 42 sts.

7th row, K14, m1, k1, m1, k12, m1, k1, m1, k14 = 46 sts.

9th row, K15, m1, k1, m1, k14, m1, k1, m1, k15 = 50 sts.

11th row, K16, m1, k1, m1, k16, m1, k1, m1, k16 = 54 sts.

13th row, K6 (m1, k1) 13 times, k16 (k1, m1) 13 times, k6

Beginning with a purl row –st. st. 9 rows

Shape Back of Head

1st row, (k8, k2tog) to end = 72 sts.

2nd row and following alternate row – Purl

3rd row, (k7, k2tog) to end = 64 sts.

5th row, (k6, k2tog) to end = 56 sts.

7th row, (k5, k2tog) to end = 48 sts.

9th row, (k4, k2tog) to end = 40 sts.

11th row, (k3, k2tog) to end = 32 sts.

13th row, (k2, k2tog) to end = 24 sts.

15th row, (k1, k2tog) to end = 16 sts.

17th row, (k2tog) to end = 8 sts.

B & T tightly

To make up Head

Join row ends, leaving a gap at centre of seam for turning and stuffing. This seam will run underneath the head. Gather round cast on sts. pull up tightly and fasten off.

Turn head right side out and stuff very firmly, taking care to push stuffing well into nose to shape it. Close gap in seam.

Ears

Make 2 pieces for each ear (2 cream, 2 brown)

Begin at top edge, cast on 16 sts.

Purl 1 row

Shape Ear

1st row, K1, m1, k to last st. m1, k1 = 18 sts.

2nd row, Purl

Repeat these two rows three times more = 22 sts.

Next row, K1, k2tog, k5 (k2tog) 3 times, k5, K2tog, k1 = 17 sts.

Cast off

Oversew the pieces together in pairs, leaving cast off edges open. Oversew cast off edges of each ear together. Sew ears in place, curving them slightly.

Body

Cast on 30 sts. in blue

Working in blue

1st row, K5, inc. into next 20 sts, k5 = 50 sts.

Beg. with a purl row, continue in st. st. and work 11 rows

Inc. to shape sides

Next row, K11 (m1, k1) 4 times, k20 (k1, m1) 4 times, k11= 58 sts.

St. st. 3 rows.

Now start to work in stripes.

2 rows gold

2 rows light brown (beige)

2 rows gold

2 rows pink

2 rows gold

2 rows green

2 rows gold

2 rows lemon

2 rows gold

2 rows red

2 rows gold

2 rows light brown

2 rows gold

2 rows pink

2 rows gold

2 rows green

2 rows gold

Body should now be long enough – Cast off

Arms

Note: There is a right and left arm. The variation for left arm is given in () brackets, otherwise the instructions are the same for both arms.

Begin at lower edge in brown.

Cast on 15 sts.

1st row, K1 (inc. in next st. k1) to end = 22 sts.

Next row, (right side) p11, k11 for right arm.

(k11, p11 for left arm)

Repeat this row 8 more times

P1 row

Change to blue wool

Shape Arm

Next row, K9, m1, k1, m1, k2, m1, k1, m1, k9 = 26 sts.

Beg. with a p row, continue in st. st. and work 33 rows

Shape top of arm

Dec. 1 st. at each end of next 4 rows

Dec. 1 st. at beginning of next 4 rows.

Next row, (k2tog) to end

B & T tightly

Sew row ends of each arm leaving top shaped edges open

Oversew across cast on sts.

Turn arms right side out and stuff

Pin open top edges of arms to sides of body with the B and T sts. 3/8ins below neck. Sew arms in place

Legs

Right leg

Begin at sole of foot in brown wool

Cast on 16 sts, mark 16 sts. with coloured wool, then cast on 8 more sts. = 24 sts.

Beg. with a purl row and continue in st. st. work 3 rows

Next row, Inc. k wise into every st. = 48 sts.

Beg. with a purl row, st. st. 2 rows

Begin foot

Beg. with a knit row, continue in st. st. and work 10 rows

Shape foot

Next row, K7 (k2tog) 10 times, k10 (k2tog) 4 times, k3 = 34 sts.

Next row, Purl

Next row, K6 (k2tog) 6 times, k16 = 28 sts.

St. st. 11 rows

Shape Leg

Knit in stripes for about 18cms.

Work in gold, k8, m1, k2, m1, k11, m1, k2, m1, k5

Purl 1 row in gold

Continue in st. st.

2 rows light brown	➔	2 rows gold
2 rows red	➔	2 rows gold
2 rows yellow	➔	2 rows gold
2 rows white	➔	2 rows gold
2 rows green	➔	2 rows gold
2 rows pink	➔	2 rows gold
2 rows light brown	➔	2 rows gold
2 rows red	➔	2 rows gold
2 rows yellow	➔	2 rows gold
2 rows white	➔	2 rows gold
2 rows green	➔	2 rows gold
2 rows pink	➔	2 rows gold
2 rows light brown	➔	2 rows gold

52 rows or approx. 18cms.

Left Leg

Begin at sole of foot in brown wool

Cast on 9sts. and mark the 9th st. with a coloured thread, then cast on 15 more sts. = 24sts.

Beg. with purl row and work 3 rows in st. st.

Next row – inc. knit wise into every st. = 48 sts.

Starting with a purl row, st. st. 2 rows

Begin foot

Beg. with a knit row, work in st. st. for 10 rows.

Shape Foot

Next row, K3 (k2tog) 4 times, k10 (k2tog) 10 times, k7 = 34sts.

Next row, Purl

Next row, K16 (k2tog) 6 times, k6 = 28sts.

St. st. 11 rows

Shape Leg

Knit in stripes

Work in gold, K5, m1, k2, m1, k11, m1, k2, m1, k8 = 32sts.

Purl 1 row

Continue in stripes in st.st.

2 rows light brown

2 rows gold

2 rows red

2 rows gold

2 rows yellow

2 rows gold

2 rows white

2 rows gold

2 rows green

2 rows gold

2 rows pink

Continue in colours for 52 rows or approx. 18cms.

Eyes (2)

Cast on 10sts. in cream

Next row, K2tog. To end of row = 5sts.

Gather sts.

Sew ends tog.

Stitch in place

Sew centre of eye with black wool

Neck Bow

Use either green or yellow wool double

Make a chain about 18ins. long

To Make Up

Head

Join row ends leaving a gap at centre of seam for turning and stuffing. This seam will run underneath the head. Gather round cast on sts. pull up tightly and fasten off.

Turn head right side out and stuff very firmly, taking care to push stuffing well into nose to shape it. Stitch gap in seam.

Body

Stitch all row ends. This seam will be at back of body. Turn right side out and stuff firmly.

To Sew Head to Body

Place head on cast on edge of body, pinning the coloured threads on head seam to the centre back seam of body.

Pin the remainder of cast on edge of body to the head where it touches. Sew in place as pinned.

Legs

Join row ends of each leg from cast on edge, leaving the top shaped edges open.

Beginning at the coloured thread at each cast on edge, oversew cast on sts. together. Turn legs right side out and stuff firmly.

The leg seam will now be at the inside leg position.

Sew legs to body.

Join centre of bottom of body between legs.

Sew arms in place.

Place ears and eyes in position.

Stitch in black wool at the end of snout.

Bib (2) Front and Back

Working in st.st. cast on 12 sts. and two colour pattern work 4 rows

Next row, dec. 1st. at each end

Purl 1 row

Next row, dec. 1st. at each end.

Purl 1 row

15 rows

Carry on in st.st. until knitting is long enough to reach to neck

Stitch 1 bib to front and 1 bib to back.

The colours on the knitting pattern are not exactly the same as Bazal's stripes, but if any knitters would like to adapt the pattern, the stripe order is as follows:

Bibliography

Attenborough, L. (1999) *When All the World's Asleep: A Children's Book of Poems, Prayers and Meditations*. Lanham, MD: Element Books.

Bliss, T. and Tetley, J. (2006) *Circle Time: A Resource Book for Primary and Secondary Schools*, 2nd edn. London: Lucky Duck .

Citizenship: A Scheme of Work For Key Stages 1 and 2. A paperback for education skills. London: QCA.

Davis, G. (1999) Six Years of Circle Time. London: Lucky Duck.

Excellence and Enjoyment: Social and Emotional Aspects of Learning (A SEAL resource). Nottingham: DfES Publications.

Powell, H. and McKee, D. (2001) *Game-Songs with Professor Dogg's Troupe*. London: A & C Black.

Mosley, J. and Murray, P. (1998) Quality Circle Time in the Primary Classroom. LDA.

Music for Chilling, *Fairy Music* (classical music by great composers inspired by fairies).

A thank you must go to all the many Circle Time writers, from whom ideas and stories have been passed down over the years and been used by all of us in our Circle Time lessons.